Introduction

This book is based on my holiday memories and other landmarks in my life, holiday diary and frequently jotted down recipes that had been passed on to me. continental flavours entranced my English taste-buds.

It was whilst on holiday in beautiful Corfu that I first met the artist Sue Bailey. We were introduced by a mutual friend, Lady Jane Barran, and I must thank her for the food, friendship and fun around the Corfiot table.

I am grateful to Dave Garner, my proof reader and Editor who has sorted out my split infinitives and controlled my occasional lapses of good taste.

As always, my husband Ted has been a tower of strength to me while I have been writing Culinary Capers. He put up with dusty skirting boards and roughly ironed shirts and was ever encouraging of my efforts.

I have always tried to see the funny side of life and I hope this is reflected in the book.

I would like to dedicate 'Culinary Capers' to my grandsons Benedict and Nathaniel Doyle. If this is my past they are our future.

Copyright Carole Wheatley 2015   ISBN 978-0-9552454-0-4

How it all Began

I first developed a love of food when I started visiting my relations in Guernsey for summer holidays. As a child growing up in post war London, I viewed food as a necessity rather than a luxury. In those days of rationing, we were eating to live rather than living to eat and we would have viewed the excesses of today with amazement.

I remember that our weekly menu didn't change much. There was always a roast on Sunday and the leftovers were used for rissoles on Monday, and cold cuts with pickle and bubble and squeak on Tuesdays. We ate fish every Friday. All our food was home cooked by my mother who sometimes cooked unusual dishes to make plain fare go further. Guernsey Bean Jar was a great favourite of mine. Food was wholesome but unexciting. I was never tempted to eat more than enough.

Guernsey had a wider range of foods than London did, and there I tasted dressed crab for the first time as a Sunday treat at teatime. We had to make a special visit to Town by bus on Saturday morning to visit the fish market. Auntie Joyce knew exactly from whom to buy it. She led us over slippery floors past stalls with live fish decorated with seaweed and shells, until we reached Mrs Ogier's stall. Her crabs and lobsters were the freshest. My Aunt chose a live chancre, which was plunged into boiling water in a vast saucepan, whose lid was weighted down with heavy rocks.

I also loved the wonderful yeasty fruit bread called Guernsey Gache. This tasted particularly good, spread with thick yellow butter after a bracing swim. Some of the foods were gathered in my aunt's back garden. We children were sent to fetch the new laid eggs for our breakfast each day. I was scared, townie that I was, of the sharp-beaked hens, but the eggs tasted so delicious that I understood that good food was something you had to take risks for. Just behind the hen house was a row of loganberry bushes. I tasted these for the first time in Guernsey. A special treat for pudding was purple loganberries spilling their juice over a bar of creamy vanilla ice cream, sprinkled with sugar. Another food that I only tasted in Guernsey was coffee ice cream, which was unavailable in Palmers Green at that time. I had my first taste of figs in Guernsey, as there was a large fig tree in the garden, which doubled as a climbing frame for children to play on. It did not produce many figs but when it did, we all sampled them.

Tomatoes featured very heavily on the bill of fare; they were free as everybody had a glut of them. We had them fried for breakfast, in sandwiches for lunch and on toast for supper. They were all vine tomatoes and were quite unlike anything one buys today from supermarkets.

When our fortnight's holiday ended, the journey home took at least twelve hours from door to door. As the ship sailed out of the harbour my heart always sank. The countryside viewed from the train from Southampton gradually gave way to urban landscape and, as we pulled into the gloomy horror of Waterloo, I thought of all that I had left behind, the cousins, the beach and the delicious foods that I would not taste for at least a year. But that little taste of 'difference' was an important experience for me and it taught me to be adventurous when I was older and went abroad and was offered more exotic foods.

Although foods from all over the world are now freely available to us I still dream of Guernsey holidays,…………coffee ice cream, a bottle of pop and dressed crab sandwiches on Sundays.

Guernsey Bean Jar

This is a winter dish and there are many variations. Until the 1920s Guernsey bean jar was the usual Guernsey breakfast. I have given my mother's recipe which I make occasionally.

Ingredients

450g (1lb) shin of beef
1 small ham hock
450g (1lb) onions
450g (1lb) carrots
450g (1lb haricot beans
Thyme, sage, parsley (plenty)

Method

Soak the beans overnight.
Place all the ingredients in an earthenware jar.
Cover with water.
Add seasonings.
Bring to the boil and simmer for 8 hours, adding more water as necessary.

How it all Began.

The Dancing Years

The German army invaded Guernsey in 1941. My parents, who were living there, were deported to Stalag Biberach where I spent my first two years. It was here from the age of eighteen months that I was first exposed to the world of dance. Two professional repertory companies were also deported from the Channel Islands and they put on regular shows for the entertainment of the inmates and the German personnel working at the camp. Teenage girls were taught to dance by the young actresses and they used to come into the room I shared and practise their dances. I would try to copy what they were doing. My first 'turn' was "The Sun Has Got His Hat On." I could only manage " 'At on. 'At on." Nevertheless, my mother knew that I was destined for the stage.

At the age of six I was taken to the Gwendolyn Perry School of Dancing. Miss Perry was a tiny, rotund, dynamic Welsh lady. She wore her hair in a chignon, and always taught ballet in high-heeled Greek- style sandals. Her studio was the dining room of her large semi-detached house, which had been stripped of furniture and carpet, and was equipped with barres, large mirrors and a polished wooden floor. The walls were adorned with ballet posters and the certificates which proclaimed that Gwendolyn Perry was a member of the Operatic Dance Society. In the corner of the room was the piano at which the pianist sat.

The highlight of my dancing year was 'A Display by the Pupils of Gwendolyn Perry.' It was held in the first week of September at Church House, Southgate, which had a stage with lights, heavy velvet curtains, lots of dressing rooms and seating for around one hundred people. It was held for two nights, Thursday and Saturday, with a Dress Rehearsal on the previous Monday. Every class performed a group number and girls who paid for private lessons were given a solo.

My first ever appearance at the age of six was as a butterfly. I found the dance a bit boring. We ran around a lot, waving our wings beside us. Every so often we would kneel with our arms behind us, fluttering. The costume was quite simple, - a sort of bathing suit made of cotton and dyed a bright colour, and a skull cap with antennae made of pipe cleaners. Butter muslin wings tie-dyed in at least three colours completed the outfit. My mother was willing to buy one dye; she would even stretch to two but she drew the line at three, so she dyed the wings in cochineal. "It is an animal dye," she explained. Unfortunately she did not set the dye and it all came off on my hands. I have a photo of me standing, pointing my toe, with my wings lifted high and my hands clenched so that I would not show the tell-tale red stains. I am wearing a grim smile. In time Miss Perry recognised my talent and I went on to win a scholarship to the London College of Dance and Drama and later ran my own Ballet School. Whenever I make Butterfly Buns, I am reminded of that anxious little girl with cochineal-stained hands.

Butterfly Buns

Buy a dozen small buns from your favourite supermarket.

Butter Cream Ingredients

75g (3oz) unsalted butter
175g (6oz) sieved icing sugar
A few drops of vanilla essence
A little milk

Method

Cream the butter until soft and fluffy.
Gradually add icing sugar and other ingredients.
Cut a thin slice off the top of each bun.
Spread butter cream on buns.
Cut slices in half to make 'wings' and push into the butter cream on the buns.
Decorate with a blob of raspberry jam if liked.

The Dancing Years.

Island Life

"The Germans have invaded? Well, thank heavens for that, it could have been the Jersey folk!" These words, probably apocryphal, certainly echoed the feelings of many of the occupants of the island of Guernsey back in 1941 when the Channel Islands became the only part of the British Isles to be invaded by the German forces. Other foes might come and go with the passing of the years, but Jersey would always be the enemy. Guernsey folk were not too keen on the English either. In 1942, after the Germans had occupied the Channel Islands for a year, an announcement from the Feldkommandatur appeared in the press ordering all men and women who were of English birth to pack a small case and leave the island for prison camps in southern Germany.

When the war was over, our family was reunited. One of my very early memories is of being carried in my father's arms to be put on the night boat-train from Waterloo to Southampton. It was November and the cold station was full of soot from the large steam locomotives. My mother was taking me 'home' to Guernsey to show me to my granny and aunts; money did not stretch to dad coming too. Mum was also going to sell the bungalow which had been built for them when they married with the help of a down payment from my mother's father. At the time he was in good health and was living with my grandmother in a tied house which went with his job but he gave my parents help to buy the bungalow on the understanding that his wife would live with them if anything happened to him. I have dim memories of sleeping in a thin cotton nightdress in a cold attic bedroom. I was not used to sleeping so far from my mother.

Two years after the end of the war, my brother was born and in time we took our annual holidays in Guernsey, staying with my granny and the aunts and cousins. By now Grandpa had died. They were wonderful holidays. The sun shone most days and if it rained we didn't care. We were allowed to go into Auntie Joyce's attic and 'make a mess'. This was a novelty for my brother and me as the plea, "Don't go making a mess!" was the order of the day at home in London. Auntie Joyce was not house proud and so we could dress up and make dens to our hearts' content.

Our best times though were on the beach. L'Ancresse was our favourite, but the wind had to be in the right direction or you got blown away. I learned to swim at L'Ancresse and I saw a nest of swallows' eggs hatch before my eyes on the common. Later, when I was fifteen, I had my first 'date' there with a choirboy from St Sampson's church. We cycled over the rolling hills watching the sun go down over the sea. I thought it was the most beautiful place in the world.

It is surprising, considering its closeness to France, that Guernsey does not have a distinctive cuisine of its own. We ate fish and the ubiquitous tomatoes of course, and sometimes we ate 'Bean Jar,' a sort of poor man's cassoulet with shin of beef and haricot beans. On the beach at tea time we often ate a slice of Guernsey Gache. This is pronounced Gosh! As a little girl I thought it was strange that we were eating a cake called Gosh. I wondered if there was another sort of cake called Blimey! My aunt bought it by the slab at Lenoure's. As my cousin Rosemary and I got older and were allowed to go to Town on our own, we were entrusted with buying the Gache. Above Lenoure's was a coffee shop, the rather grand Guernsey equivalent of a 'greasy spoon' where young people of the opposite sex used to gather to look at one another and make disparaging remarks.

Coffee and a slice of Guernsey Gache thickly spread with butter was our idea of heaven and, when in London we became homesick for Guernsey, this is what my mother would make for us...

Guernsey Gache

Ingredients

700g (1½ lbs) plain flour
225g (½ lb) butter
2 eggs, beaten
450g (1lb) sultanas or currants
110g (4oz) mixed peel
1 sachet dried yeast
150ml (¼ pint) milk
50g (2oz) sugar
pinch of salt

Method

Grease a 2lb cake or loaf tin.
Cream the butter with the sugar.
Gradually add the beaten eggs and the flour.
Warm the milk to blood heat.
Sprinkle the yeast over the cake mixture and add the warm milk.
Mix well, adding all the fruit as you mix.
Knead, as you would bread, for 5 minutes until all the fruit is incorporated and the dough feels springy to the touch.
Cover with a floured tea towel and leave to rise for 2 hours in a warm room.
Knead again (knock-back) and turn into the prepared tin.
Leave to rise again for approximately half an hour while the oven heats up.
Bake in a moderate oven 180°C (gas mark 5) for 1 hour, or until golden.

Childhood Christmas Memories

"Who is that naughty little girl?"

That was the voice of my headmistress, Miss Punchard, and she was looking straight at me. It was the dress rehearsal of our Reception Class Nativity Play and I was playing an angel. It wasn't a demanding part. All I was required to do was kneel beside the crib with my arms crossed over my chest for twenty minutes. But I had committed a cardinal sin. I had fidgeted for twenty minutes. I had hoped for a better part: Mary, the Angel Gabriel, or even an attendant to a King, but, in 1948, little girls were offered very few places to display their talent.

Luckily it did not spoil my Christmas. There was the church Carol Service to look forward to and making paper chains and, of course, the wonderful Christmas Dinner. Food was plain and limited after the war. I did not see a banana until I was five years old. On Christmas Day, after the church service, we always had a chicken or a capon, with stuffing and an array of vegetables. This was followed by my mother's Christmas pudding made to her mother's recipe. There was no brandy butter in those days. Brandy was reserved for treating my Granny's palpitations so the pudding was served with custard, which I always refused.

My mother and my aunt in Guernsey always exchanged parcels and there was great excitement when the 'Guernsey Parcel' arrived. Inside, there were presents wrapped in Christmas paper which were kept until Christmas Day - a packet of Collins Guernsey Sweets – mixed boiled sweets only available in Guernsey – and a homemade Christmas pudding. There was ongoing competition between my mother and my aunt. On opening the parcel mother would always exclaim, "Oh Eddie! Look! My pudding is darker than Joyce's." 'Dark' implied superior ingredients.

In time I grew up and was eventually chosen to be Mary in the Nativity Play. I also sang a solo in the Coventry Carol. We were now better off and had turkey for Christmas Dinner. Dad would not let us call it lunch as it was the main meal of the day. Our meal was timed to be over before the King spoke to us on the wireless set.

When I married, I tried to keep Christmas magic alive and stirring up the Christmas pudding was part of our family tradition. We went carolling around the village and exchanged parcels with our Canadian cousins. Our daughter was born on Christmas Day and, in time, gave birth to her own baby just before Christmas. In latter years my very elderly mother would always spend Christmas Day with us. She brought home-made mince pies and a dozen coffee éclairs, which were her speciality. She did not really enjoy being with us as our house was too cold and our lunch timing was too laid back. As it was our daughter's birthday, we always had a glass of champagne to toast her at 11 a.m. and then she opened her birthday presents. One particular year I remember mother's plaintive words, "Don't forget the Queen! We are going to miss the Queen!" ringing like a leitmotiv as Ted and I tried to put the finishing touches to the meal. Eventually, in absolute exasperation I said, "Oh Mum! B----- the Queen!" completely undoing my promise to God at the Midnight Mass that I would not lose my temper with my mother on Christmas Day and fulfilling Miss Punchard's words that I was a naughty little girl. I could give you my mother's Christmas pudding recipe but most people have their own family speciality. Instead I will give you a delicious root vegetable dish which was given to me by my friend and neighbour Susan. I usually serve this at Christmas, especially when we have vegetarian guests.

You can always watch the Queen in the evening. Or miss her for once.

Root Vegetable Crush

Ingredients

700g (1½ lbs) celeriac
4 large carrots
2 tablespoons horseradish sauce
142ml double cream
2 tablespoons parmesan cheese, grated

Method

Peel the vegetables and cut into smallish chunks.
Cook in lightly salted water until soft.
Mash lightly with a fork, stir in horseradish sauce.
Turn into a buttered ovenproof dish.
Pour the cream over the top and mix gently.
Sprinkle with parmesan cheese.

Bake at 190ºC (gas mark 5) for 25 – 30 mins.

Childhood Christmas Memories

Church Times

Growing up in the London suburbs my social life during the forties and fifties tended to revolve around the Church's year. My mother, brother and I were regular church-goers. I was in the Brownies, then the Guides. Later, I acted in the church drama group and joined the youth club. My brother was a chorister and an altar server. My father was not a regular church goer until a new parish priest came and started a Glee Club. Dad, a tenor, joined and was gradually absorbed into the family of the church.

Apart from Christmas there were several exciting annual occasions for us to look forward to. One was the Vicar's Garden Party in June. As a member of the Gwendoline Perry School of Dancing I was often chosen to dance on the grass. A difficult manoeuvre if you are trying to perform the Irish Jig on uneven turf. The refreshments were rather plain. There were curly white sandwiches with luncheon meat or cheese and pickle and an assortment of cakes. Strong 'builders brew' tea was poured from large brown enamel tea-pots. There was always a raffle and one memorable year I won a beautiful draped doll's cot with a gauze canopy and mauve flower-sprigged bedding. It was far beyond my wildest dreams.

In September we had a Harvest Supper. In November there was a Christmas Bazaar. We were a suburban church with a very large church hall, which was marked out for a badminton court with a smaller meeting room next to the kitchen. It was in this room that we had the Harvest Supper. Entry was by ticket only but I do not remember anyone being turned away. The menu was the same every year. One of the parishioners bought a very large ham which his wife cooked. It was then carved into the requisite number of slices and served with hot buttered potatoes and a green salad. On every table there was the inevitable dish of beetroot in vinegar and a jar of salad cream. Mayonnaise was unheard of in Bowes Park in the fifties. The ladies of the Mothers Union and the Young Wives made the puddings, the same choices every year. There was apple pie and cream or lemon meringue pie. My mother always made a lemon meringue pie. She made her own pastry of course, but always made the filling from a packet of Royal's Lemon Meringue Pie Filling. This powdery substance contained a gelatine capsule full of lemon essence. You mixed it with boiling water, ensured the capsule and its contents were fully dissolved and then added a beaten egg yolk and put whisked egg white on top. It was alright, but not as good as those made from scratch.

The Christmas Bazaar in November was a racier affair and took place in the large church hall which was decked out in bunting. There were notices entreating you to 'Shop Early for Christmas!' Profits went to the church fund. When my brother and I were very young my father gave us each half a crown to spend at the Bazaar in addition to the money we had saved from our pocket money. There were lots of attractions such as Hoop La, a Bottle stall, a Cake stall, Lucky Dip and Grand Draw. There were also stalls selling knitted baby clothes, bed socks, hot water bottle covers and lavender bags. I usually managed to buy a Christmas present for my mother at the Bazaar. When I was in my late teens, in the early sixties, another girl and I decided to run a Bazaar Boutique. We bought lots of pairs of skimpy panties, made some bright scarves and garters and asked the local Chemist's shop to donate bubble bath and shampoo. We did not make a large profit, but we covered our costs with a little over and generated some interest from the younger members of the congregation.

In the evening there was a Bazaar Buffet. Here you could choose from a series of dishes and my mother usually made Salmon and Mushroom Pie. I often make it when we want a quick supper dish. It is good with oven chips or a baked potato.

Salmon and Mushroom Pie

Ingredients

225g (8oz) shortcrust pastry
A tin of Campbell's condensed mushroom soup
Large tin of pink or red salmon
Beaten egg to glaze

Method

Turn oven to 220°C (200°C fan) gas mark 7.
Roll pastry thinly and use half to line a 7 inch (12.5 cm) pie dish.
Chill lined pie dish for 20 minutes.
Drain and flake salmon, remove bones but reserve liquid.
Combine salmon with condensed mushroom soup.
Add a little of the reserved salmon liquid.
Pour mixture into flan tin.
Roll remaining pastry and cover mixture, seal the edges with water.
Make a small hole in the top of the pie.
Glaze the top with beaten egg.
Bake for 10 minutes and then reduce the temperature to 200°C (180°C fan), gas mark 6 for 20 minutes.

The Coronation Pageant

Most London schools celebrated the Queen's Coronation in some way. My class was chosen from St Michael at Bowes Junior School to take part in a Pageant which was written by a local historian and was called, 'The Three Elizabeths.' It was performed in a large arena in a local park. Many children from other schools in the Borough also took part but we did not meet until the final performance.

Our class played Tudor peasants and we were coached to mime buying and selling as if we were in a Tudor market place. Each of us had to invent a character and act within that part. We did not simply 'run around' but really portrayed a market scene. We were given a sketch of the costume we were to wear. The girls had to wear rolls around their waists tied with tapes to make their skirts stand out. I think the technical term is farthingale. We then wore long skirts, laced bodices and white blouses. Long hair had to be plaited and worn at the front, bound with tapes not ribbons. My mother excelled herself as she found some old brocade curtains and dyed them bottle green. My farthingale was made fom my dad's old socks stuffed and tied around my waist where they nestled comfortably above my green school knickers, I felt like 'The Cat's Whiskers.' A proper costume at last!

The Pageant was long and complicated. Good Queen Bess was played by an eighteen-year old sixth former called Josie who rode a horse side saddle. The Queen's speech at Tilbury (spoken by Josie) was most impressive and we all shouted "Hosah!" (the Elizabethan form of "Hurrah.") Then came our market scene. While we were acting a boy all dressed in green twigs and foliage came around kissing the girls. He was 'Jack in the Green' a well-known character at Tudor fairs. To my joy he chose to kiss me, twice! I felt I must look really special in my bottle green dress. I learned much later that pubs called 'The Green Man' were also named after him. The climax of the Pageant was the Narrator saying…… "and now let time stand still as…….." and all the performers ran into the large arena as the music, 'Oh God our Help in Ages Past' was played. At this point we were told to stand stock still. It was the climax of the performance and any movement WOULD SPOIL THE WHOLE PAGEANT. I was an obedient little girl. So as my skirt began to fall down because my mother's stitching had come undone I stood stock still; and all would have been well, it was lodged on my father's socks, if my friend Pauline hadn't disobeyed the stand still rule and pulled my skirt to the ground revealing my green school knickers. An important day ruined forever for me because of my mother's refusal to fasten off properly.

Quick Coronation Chicken

Ingredients

1 cooked chicken
1 onion chopped and fried until soft
Grated rind of a lemon
1 tbsp curry paste
3 tbsp mayonnaise
1 tbsp mango chutney
½ jar of apricot jam

Method

Remove chicken from carcass and shred into small chunks.
Mix mayonnaise, apricot jam, curry paste and lemon rind together.
Fold chicken into mixture.
Serve with rice or a baked potato
This is lovely for a summer picnic.

Coronation Pageant

Farandole

When I was twenty one, after working for three years in local government, I won a scholarship to the London College of Dance and Drama which was then part of the Arts Educational Trust. We were around 70 students, all girls, residing in a beautiful old house in Addison Road, West London. It was known as the 'Peacock House' and had formerly been the private residence of the Debenham family. Peacock House was a magnificent stately home with large drawing rooms and dining and breakfast rooms which were used as dance studios. A wooden staircase led to a galleried first floor where there were lecture rooms and a library, together with some bedrooms for staff and the second and third year students. The first year students slept at the top of the house in what would have been the maids' bedrooms. Down in the basement there was a kitchen and dining room, a laundry and a large squash court which was used for dancing classes.

We had a Ballet class every day and learned various other forms of dance such as Modern Stage, Tap and Classical Greek throughout the week. My favourite subject was National Dance. In this subject we learned dances from all over Europe and the then USSR. Some of these were solo dances, some were couple dances and others were group dances involving the whole class. One of the group dances that we learned in our first term was the Farandole, a winding chain dance from Brittany. We usually danced this in the large squash court as there was plenty of space. The whole class joined hands and followed the leader who led them in a winding chain around the room. After a few bars of music she led them in even walking steps into a maze-like formation (a bit like a swiss roll). When the leader reached the centre of the 'maze' she had to unwind from the maze in one of two ways. She either turned around lifting her hand and the hand of the girl next to her so that all the rest of the chain passed under their arms. Alternatively, she went under the arches of the rest of the chain and they all followed until the whole chain became a circle and broke into a springing dance travelling to the left. It was vital that nobody broke the chain. Everything went horribly wrong if hands were not kept firmly clasped.

One memorable day I was chosen to lead the Farandole. What an honour! All went well at first. Winding into the maze went without a hitch. Then it was time to unwind. I turned lifting the arm of my friend Stella, and she and I led the rest of the chain out into a long line. I got a bit over ambitious at this stage and decided to repeat the maze and then come out under the arches. Excitement may have made me speed up, or else the pianist upped the tempo. I can't be sure. I chose two girls to be my exit arches, indicating with a lift of the eyebrows and suddenly I was leading the rest of the line along to the climax of the dance. Unfortunately one of the arches, Judy, forgot that she had to turn under the arch too and ended up with her arms across her chest like a strait jacket. With a look of terror she carried on dancing. She didn't break the chain. Several girls started tittering and, aware that something was wrong behind me, I began to dance too quickly. You must have a strong anchor person at the back of a Farandole and unfortunately the back of the line swung out like a whip. Girls knocked against the wall, others danced through the resin box, Judy's strait jacket threatened to throttle her. But nobody broke the chain.

"Stop the music!!" called our teacher. "That is the worst Farandole I have seen in twenty years teaching. Carole Ashton managed to make the Farandole look dangerous!"

Then seeing my downcast face she said, "At least nobody broke the chain. Time for lunch girls."

I don't dance the Farandole these days, but I do cook French Onion Tart from Brittany. I hope you enjoy it too.

French Onion Tart

Ingredients

175g (6oz) short crust pastry
450g (1lb) white onions
28g (1oz) butter, 1 tablespoon olive oil
1 large egg
4 tablespoons double cream
1 teaspoon sugar
Salt and pepper
8 anchovies, rinsed and dried

Method

Turn oven to 200°C (180°C fan) Gas mark 6.
Put a baking sheet in the oven to heat.
Grease a 9 inch 7)7.5 cm loose bottomed flan tin.
Roll pastry and line the tin. Chill for ten minutes.
Then bake blind for 10 mins using baking beans.
Remove baking beans, seal the pastry with a thin wash of beaten egg and bake for 10 mins.
Meanwhile, chop the onions finely and fry very slowly in the butter and oil until soft and golden.
Keep a lid on the pan whilst frying the onions.
Add sugar, salt and pepper and allow the onions to caramelise.
Remove from the heat, and allow to cool slightly.
Beat the egg with the cream and pour it over the onions.
Pour the eggy mixture into the flan tin.
Place the flan tin on the heated baking sheet, decorate with anchovies and bake for 30 minutes or until set.

Dancing Tears

Three Girls on a Bummel

It was the sixties. The 6-day war was raging in Israel. The Beatles were breaking new ground in the world of pop music and Juliet, Liz and I decided to take Germany by storm.

Why Germany? Well I had been born there but had never been back. Liz had read 'Three Men on A Bummel' and thought it was very funny whilst Juliet had heard that Germany was cleaner than France and that the cakes were better.

So off we went. We were all around twenty and very innocent. As trainee dancing teachers we were more aware of folk dancing in different lands than world shattering events like the war in Vietnam or the division of Germany. We were travelling on a shoestring, so we decided that we would have to hitchhike some of the time, and only when necessary, use local trains.

We each brought different skills to the group. Liz had travelled more extensively than the rest of us and spoke fairly good German. Juliet, the youngest, was very good with money. She worked out the budget and decided when we were allowed a cake. I was twenty one. Quite old compared to the others. I knew the ways of the world, having worked for three years in local government. I decided what we bought for our picnic lunches and organised the washing of the plates. (Honestly the others were awful! They would have put them back in their rucksacks without a wipe!) I also had the most responsible task of deciding *who it would be safe to take a lift from*. I would stand a few yards back from the road looking into cars. If the driver looked decent and upstanding I would signal to the other two and we would then stick thumbs up for a lift.

All went well until we reached Cologne and there was no room in the very large Youth Hostel. The next hostel was a long way away and we were too late to get there by the required 4 p.m. deadline. As we were deliberating a young man approached us. He spoke fairly good English although he was clearly Arabic. He offered us a lift in his friend's car to a cheap hotel. Juliet was alarmed. She viewed all foreigners with suspicion, but as Liz and I said, there were three of us and only two of them, so we accepted. The two Palestinians were called Elias and Khalid. They were studying in Germany and were very charming and helpful. As they dropped us off Elias said "We know the cheap places to eat; shall we pick you up later and take you around?"

They took us to a Bierkeller which was full of students of all different nationalities. There was dancing and conversation was difficult over the loud music. Elias kept winking at me so I felt it only polite to wink back from time to time. I thought it might be an Arabic custom. I didn't want him to think I was being stand-offish. After a while he invited me outside for some air. When we got into the moonlight he whispered to me, "You, me,… after the dancing. We *go* together?" "Go where?" I asked. "We go to the bed?" urged Elias, his breath coming hot and strong. "No, certainly not!" I replied. "I am not that sort of girl" "All English girls go to the bed" replied Elias darkly. "Well I don't" I replied, "and neither do my friends". When we got back inside I realised that what I took to be a wink was in fact an involuntary twitch. I had been sending out the wrong signals completely.

The next day the young men drove us to the station so that we could check into a youth hostel well before opening time. As we were coming to the end of our adventure in Germany we felt we could afford 'Kaffee und Kuchen' in a small Konditorei, a specialist coffee house. The recipe below, given me by my German teacher Jutta Austen, might well have been on the menu.

Almond and Orange Torte

Ingredients

1 medium orange
3 medium eggs
225g (8oz) caster sugar
250g (9oz) ground almonds
½ tsp baking powder
Icing sugar to dust

Method

Grease and base line an 8 inch (20.5cm) spring form cake tin.
Put whole orange in a small saucepan, cover with water.
Bring to the boil, cover and simmer for at least an hour until tender.
Remove from the water and leave to cool.
Cut orange in half and remove pips.
Whizz in a food processor to make a purée.
Preheat the oven to 180°C (fan 160°C) gas mark 4.
Put the caster sugar and eggs in a bowl and whisk together until thick and pale.
Fold in the almonds, baking powder and orange purée.
Pour the mixture into the tin.
Bake for 40 – 50 minutes until a skewer comes out clean.
Leave to cool in the tin then remove the cake, peel off the lining paper and place on a serving plate.
Dust with icing sugar.

This may be served with crème fraiche.

3 girls on a Bummel

Theatrical Disappointments

I used to sing with a local amateur operatic society and suffered a keen disappointment. I was not chosen to be a fairy in 'Iolanthe', a story of fairies and peers. Just before the auditions the Director said "Anyone can try for the role of fairy. Fairies come in all ages, sizes and shapes," so I felt confident of getting a fairy role. However, to my sorrow everyone over sixty or over size sixteen was chosen to be a suffragette. The Director delivered the news in the following way.

"The following ladies will be fairies," she announced reading out a list. A sigh of relief passed around all those on it. "I have something very special for the rest of you," she smiled. You will be suffragettes and I have written you each a line to say in Act 2. Fairies, you will wear white tights, suffragettes you will wear black ones. Fairies, you will wear silver sparkly nail varnish; suffragettes, you won't". We non fairies had the pleasure of singing off-stage with the fairies and onstage with the men. We sang the tenor part an octave higher. In fact we were tenors without the usual appendages. It was a great disappointment.

It is not the first time that I have had my fairy dreams thwarted. When I was seven I was not chosen to be 'Airy Fairy' in the church junior drama group production of 'Why the Fuchsia Hangs its Head'.

"We do not think you are fairy material dear," I was told, "but we would like you to play 'Bright Sprite'. We think that would be more suited to your talents". I wanted to wear the fairy dress and the gauzy wings, but instead my mother had to make me a Sprite's dress. I had to say, "My name is Bright Sprite in my frock there's every hue, yellow, red and violet, pink and green and blue". You will notice that he rhyme implies *six* colours. *Six* rolls of crepe paper. My mother, repeating her 'cochineal is an animal dye' trick, would only buy red, blue and yellow, insisting that if I kept moving no one would notice that the other colours were not there.

There was one time when I did get invited to be a fairy, though more by default than choice. I was asked to perform 'Nobody Wants a Fairy When She's Forty', as a surprise at someone's 40th birthday party. It was a large, posh affair and I was to perform in a marquee on New Year's Eve. I had to hide between the outer and inner layers of the marquee while the guests came in, then jump out, shout "Surprise!" and then sing the song. It was not an unqualified success. My husband, who was accompanying me on the piano, lost the music and played dull keyboard harmony. This makes everything sound like a hymn; the joke fell a bit flat.

I failed to get the part of Titania in my school production of 'A Midsummer Night's Dream', but at the end of my first year at Drama school, an all-girl establishment, we performed 'Electra', a Greek tragedy. I wanted to be part of the Chorus and declaim, "Discord within dividing child from child", but someone had to play King Aegisthus, (someone who was not fairy material). This honour fell to me. But here's the rub. Even with a false beard and a staff to help me walk from the hip in a masculine way I still couldn't be convincing as a man. "I don't know why she cast you in that role," said a friend. "You are a *characte*r actress not a dramatic actress". Of course! I have never again yearned to be a fairy. A character actress suits me fine.

Fairy Cakes

Ingredients

110g (4oz) self-raising flour
110g (4oz) butter, softened
110g (4oz) caster Sugar
50g (2oz) currants or sultanas
2 eggs, lightly beaten

Method

Pre-heat oven to 190°C, gas mark 5.
Cream the butter and sugar until soft and light.
Add eggs a little at a time.
Sift the flour and gently fold into the mixture.
Fold in the currants or sultanas.
Place 18 paper baking cases into bun trays.
Spoon in the mixture, filling about two-thirds of the cases.
Bake for 20-25 minutes, or until well risen and golden brown.
Place on a wire rack to cool.
Makes 18

Nobody wants a fairy when she's forty
`Theatrical Disappointments'

Ivy

My mother-in-law was called Ivy which means 'a clinging creeper' but she longed to be called Myfanwy which means 'my fair one'. She was sandwiched between two brothers and had three sons, and longed for feminine company. A faithful member of both the W.I. and the Townswomen's Guild she was an exceptionally good craftswoman. She sang bass (yes bass!) in the W.I. choir. From 1964 onwards Ivy always wore trousers, unusual for a woman in her seventies, eighties and nineties. I had a very good relationship with her because I never tried to compete and the only time that we had a small spat was when my husband Ted (her third son) innocently remarked, "You are an excellent cook Mother, but Carole makes better scrambled eggs than you." She was outraged.

Ivy was a very proud mother. "I have two wonderful sons…..and Ted" she would tell people. Her first two sons were a doctor and a scientist respectively. Ted was 'only a teacher.' She never quite forgave him for moving from a teaching post in a Grammar school to head of a Primary school. She was particularly proud of her first son, Michael, who was a doctor in Canada. Once she fainted on Brighton station and a doctor was called. As Ivy regained consciousness she looked into his face and whispered, "My son is a doctor."

Ivy was a wonderful mother-in-law to me and came to the rescue when I was very ill following the birth of my first child. My mother was so upset by my ill-health that she was unable to be of any help to me. They were very dark days for me, but Ivy pulled me through and I have never forgotten her strength at a time when I was so weak.

During the Second World War Ivy and her sons were evacuated to Oxford where she made many friends. Some she liked more than others. On one occasion she saw one of these new acquaintances, Mrs Parker, walking up the path and, too busy to entertain her, she stood quietly in the drawing room hoping she would go away. To her surprise the woman went around to the back door which was unlocked, opened it and began calling, "Ivy!" "Ivy!" Mother crept up to her bedroom. To her horror she heard her unwelcome guest climbing the stairs still calling, "Ivy!" "Are you there?" In dismay mother hid under the bed and heard Mrs Parker going around opening drawers and examining the things on the dressing table. When she told the story afterwards she said that if Mrs Parker had bent down and found her under the bed she would have said, "Just doing some deep dusting!"

I met her for the first time when Ted and I were an item but not yet engaged. Ivy and her husband Pat hosted a garden party for Michael and his wife who were visiting from Canada with two of the grandchildren. Ted's other brother, cousins, their spouses and offspring gathered in Seaford for a reunion lunch. I was rather nervous. I was fifteen years younger than most of the cousins and nine years younger than Ted who was the youngest child of the Wheatley family. Some of the grandchildren and great nieces were nearly as old as me. I was not quite sure where I fitted into this large family. Ivy prepared a buffet lunch of cold meats, poached salmon, various salads and delicious puddings. The most memorable for me was Ivy's Almond Dessert. I often make it for special occasions.

Of course I could have given you my recipe for scrambled eggs………

Almond Dessert (quick and easy)

Ingredients

1 jam Swiss roll (no cream please)
50g (2oz) unsalted butter
50g (2oz) caster sugar
50g (2oz) ground almonds
Some sherry
Flaked almonds, toasted
275ml (½ pint) of thick Birds Custard made with whole milk
Angelica or glacé cherries

Method

Line a pretty dish with sliced Swiss roll. Soak it with a little sherry.
Make ½ pint of thick Birds Custard. Allow to cool.
Mix the butter, sugar and ground almonds into the cooled custard.
Beat until it is like smooth cream.
Pile over the sponge and decorate with toasted almonds and glace cherries if liked.
You can serve this with cream, but I think that is overkill.

Ivy

A Taste of Hell

It was the late 60's. I was young, newly married and giving my first ever dinner party at our tiny house in Twickenham. In those early days my husband was a better cook than me. But I had a plastic covered book entitled 'MY RECIPES' in which I methodically copied out anything new that I mastered. I was determined to excel on the culinary front.

I cannot remember all the guests who came to dinner that night, although I do remember that we had invited a young Indian man, Kishore, who was studying in England. He seemed a little lonely. We knew that he was a vegetarian and in those days this was very unusual. We had one other friend who was vegetarian and she seemed to exist on omelettes and nut cutlets. Luckily Ted had spent some time living with a family in Bombay who ran a chain of restaurants known as the Chhaya restaurants. Here he had learned to make Chhaya Chops, a vegetable cutlet which we nicknamed Bombay Balls. Ted taught me to make it during our brief engagement, (teaching me to cook was part of his courting ritual). It isn't a difficult dish to cook and is very cheap to make, consisting mostly of boiled lentils and vegetables. Some cheese is added to give flavour and help the amino acid content. The whole mixture is bound together with eggs before frying. I had made a crème caramel for dessert.

The table was laid; I was ready in my Mary Quant mini-dress and my bare-look lipstick. Ted was dashingly attired in his black corduroy jacket. The doorbell rang.

The guests arrived and we offered them all a sherry. "No thank-you Mrs Wheatley, " said Kishore, "I am a Hindu and I abstain from liquor." In time we moved into the dining room. The starter was something like half a grapefruit with a glace cherry on it, considered quite outré in the sixties. During the course of the conversation I said to Kishore, "I understand that you are a vegetarian". His reply made my heart stand still. "I am a vegan Mrs Wheatley; I eat neither meat, fish, eggs nor cheese".

Oh no! There goes the main course and the pudding! Ted, sophisticated, worldly-wise and shameless mouthed to me, "Don't say anything!" and for once I obeyed.

As we went into the kitchen to bring in the Bombay Balls I said to Ted, "What are we going to do? Everything has eggs in. If he eats them he'll go to Hell!" Ted's reply amazed me. "Don't be ridiculous Carole! There is no Hell."

There is no Hell! I had been married to him for a month, we had known each other for a year and only now did I know that for Ted 'Hell' was a swear-word not a reality. Kishore ate the Bombay Balls with relish. "These are most delicious Mrs Wheatley. There is a flavour that I cannot quite identify......" "That will be the mixed herbs", I said looking him straight in the eye, "and the seasoning."

I lied with such composure that I surprised myself. I'd been such a goody-goody wimp until then. But the thought that there might not be a Hell was so releasing.

I didn't let him eat the crème caramel, "It's got eggs in, " I explained. "Won't you have some fruit instead?" Not just a liar, but devious too!

I still have the book of 'MY RECIPES' and I have copied out Bombay Balls. I hope you enjoy them more than I did that first time I made them back in 1968.

Bombay Balls

Ingredients

450g (1lb) lentils
900g (2lbs) onions (peeled and chopped)
1 carrot (peeled and sliced)
2 eggs beaten
1 heaped teaspoon curry powder
28g (1oz) hard cheese, grated
3 tbsps olive oil
1 tbsp mixed herbs
Salt and pepper
2 tablespoons golden breadcrumbs or flour

Method

Boil onions carrots and lentils for about half an hour until the vegetables are soft.
Strain and use the liquid as Dhal soup.
Place a little oil in a frying pan. Add the boiled onions, carrots and lentils.
Heat over a slow heat to let the remaining moisture evaporate.
Add grated cheese, beaten egg, herbs and seasoning stirring continuously.
Continue on low heat until mixture becomes dough like.
Empty onto a plate and leave to cool.
Divide the mixture into 24 small balls, flatten slightly to form patties, coat with beaten egg and breadcrumbs or flour.
Fry in batches.
These are delicious hot or cold. Serve with crisp green salad or rice.
The Chhaya restaurant made them in the shape of a lamb chop and served them with a mixed salad.

Last Tango Near Paris

When did you last dance the tango? If you are an English man you will probably reply, "Never" or "The what?" If you are an English woman you may have learned to dance it at school but you will almost certainly, like me, have learned to dance it with another girl. I always had to dance the man's part because I was flat chested and tall for my age.

If you are German or French you may well have danced the tango last week or last night. You will have learned it at a family party or wedding when you were about six years old. Your granny will have taught you, or an aunt. You will be as confident in your dancing as you are in your kissing, which you will have learned at the age of fourteen, advised by an older woman (probably not your granny, although I cannot be sure about that).

I last danced the tango in 1978 in a village near Paris. It was the occasion of a twinning ceremony between East Bergholt and Barbizon. On the final night of our stay there was a party for 'Tout Le Monde', where we were treated to a vast buffet with dishes provided by each of our hostesses. It was here I tasted Barbizon pâté for the first time.

The meal was followed by dancing. I was invited to dance by an exquisite Frenchman called Yves. It was the tango.

"I'm not sure if I can do it", I confessed "I usually dance man".

He lifted one eyebrow and said, "Madame, surrender yourself to me."

I surrendered.

I can still remember the excitement of that dance. He was an excellent dancer and it was impossible to go wrong as he gave such a good lead. Twice around the dance floor he got very ambitious and threw me over his leg. How I wished I'd changed out of my flat lace-up shoes! All eyes were on us and I glanced around to see if my husband was watching and taking note. I caught sight of him on the other side of the dance floor attempting to dance with the lady mayor of Barbizon. Although she was very slim and chic he looked as if he was driving a heavy goods vehicle. She wore a slightly pained expression.

I have never danced the tango since then, but I'm up for offers; telephone number supplied on request.

We have been on many European holidays and watched how European men dance. The middle-aged Germans have nearly all been to dancing classes and can perform the rumba, samba and tango with great style. The older Germans hold their women as if they are cuddling a beer barrel, but that is alright because beer is precious to them. The Frenchmen work on the principle of "If I'm not with the girl I love, I love the girl I'm with". English men stamp on your feet and dance off the beat. I cannot count how many times I've had to dance the waltz to the counts 2, 3, 1, while being told the latest cricket score.

If going fully into the European Union means that our men will pick up some tips on that delicate art of foreplay which is social dancing a lot of English women will be very happy.

It seems strange to think we fought the French on and off for nine hundred years. The tango is so much better. It's not so much a contest, - more of a surrender.

Barbizon Pâté

Ingredients

225g (8oz) lean minced beef
450g (1lb) fat belly pork, minced
450g (1lb pigs liver), minced
100ml (4 fluid oz) dry white wine
25ml (1 fluid oz) brandy
2 cloves garlic, crushed
6 black peppercorns
6 juniper berries
175g (6oz) streaky bacon, chopped
1 level teaspoon salt
¼ teaspoon ground mace
900g (2lb) loaf tin or terrine

Method

Place meats in a large bowl with the chopped bacon and mix thoroughly.
Add the salt, mace, juniper berries and crushed garlic.
Pour alcohol over, mix well, and leave for several hours.
Pour mixture into the loaf tin, place in a bain-marie half full of hot water and bake in a moderate oven, 180°C (gas mark 4) for 1 ½ hours.
Cool in the tin and press with weights before turning out.

Last Tango

Hebden Bridge

When our children were five and seven we were offered the use of a cottage in Yorkshire for our annual holidays. It belonged to a teacher friend and lay just outside Hebden Bridge, 8 miles west of Halifax on the confluence of the rivers Calder and Hebden. The cottage lay above Hebden Bridge in a former mill village called Pecket Well which had some connection to Thomas à Beckett – but I can't remember what.

The journey from East Bergholt was quite stressful with two small children and a dog, but we used to break it by stopping at Sherwood Forest for a picnic lunch. We are both rather absent minded and one year we drove off and left the dog at the picnic stop. We did not miss her for about 20 miles; then our small daughter suddenly observed from the back seat, "Oh poor Jemima!" We then made the difficult journey back to find her sitting patiently awaiting our return.

I think our thoughtlessness must have put a jinx on the holiday for on that occasion it rained almost every day. On our arrival we crossed the road and went into the nearby fields to stretch our legs after the long journey. The grass was a little slippery so I tried to hold our small daughter's hand, only to have her refuse. In exasperation I gave her a little push and she fell over. It was a very small push, but although I tried to apologise she was furious. "I don't like ladies who push little girls over, " she announced. She would not let me kiss her goodnight for the rest of the holiday.

The cottage had only one small bedroom where the children slept, so my husband and I bunked down on the floor of the sitting room with the dog. There was a bathroom and a downstairs living room with a small kitchen. There was also a dusty cellar which in earlier days probably housed coal. Our children found this grimy place fascinating. Whenever we arrived Jenny would find a duster (kept in the cellar) and clean the house from top to toe before making a little den for her doll to sleep in. Most of the cottages had formerly been mill workers' homes. The key to the cottage was kept by a farmer's wife and we became very friendly with her family over the years. Audrey and her husband had run a small family farm but were now retired. They still had one cow and told me they drank a gallon of full cream milk a day.

The weather could not be relied upon in Yorkshire but we always had great fun. We walked vast stretches of the Pennine Way and despite the children and the dog we were always allowed into country pubs. Our children loved damming up streams and helping their father make camp fires where he would cook sausages and beans. In the evenings we would play cards or monopoly and read as there was no television. As the children got older we often made excursions into Hebden Bridge which became more and more interesting through the 70's and 80's. It had a small theatre and many independent coffee shops, cafés, artisan bakers and several fish and chip shops. We sometimes bought Eccles cakes which were a local speciality. In time we could afford to take more expensive holidays further afield but we all look back on those Yorkshire holidays with nostalgia.

Eccles Cakes

Ingredients

A packet of frozen puff pastry thawed

Filling

25g (1oz) of butter
110g (4oz) currants
A little mixed peel, chopped
25g (1oz) of sugar

Method

Roll pastry on a lightly floured surface and cut into circles 9 cms (3½ inches) across with a plain cutter.
Mix filling ingredients together and place a teaspoon of the filling mixture into the centre of each circle.
Damp the edges of pastry and draw up and pinch together to enclose filling.
Turn cakes over and flatten with a rolling pin so that the currants just show through.
Cut three slits in each cake.
Brush with water and sprinkle with sugar.
Bake at 200ºC (gas mark 7) for about 15 minutes until golden.

"I don't like ladies who push little girls

Convent Days

Once my children had started school I was employed as a drama teacher by a private Convent school in Colchester. I had had little to do with Catholics until my appointment. I knew about the 'no meat on Friday rule' of course. When I was at College two of my friends were RC. And whenever there was a Friday night party nearly all the food was forbidden to them. My mother, a high Anglican, was always threatening to convert to Catholicism as she believed that the Church of England was born out of lust and depravity. Luther and the Reformation had completely passed her by.

It was with some trepidation that I applied for the job in the Convent. I worried. If appointed would I inadvertently swear, or worse, blaspheme? I soon discovered the nuns to be warm, strong, interesting women and I really enjoyed my time there. The academic standards were high, but the curriculum was rather narrow, which was one of the reasons I asked the Head if Mr Silly could visit.

My husband was head of a Village Primary school. He was invited by the Suffolk Library Service to dress up as Mr Silly (from the Mr Men books). He then led a long line of children from Christchurch Park in Ipswich to the Library where he read them a Mr Men story. The brightly coloured costume was very impressive. It was larger than life size and his eyes peeped out from the fat stomach while his torso and head towered above. I thought it would be great if he could come to the school where I was teaching the next day and read to the children at break time.

It was agreed that the whole school would be sitting in the hall waiting for the 'surprise visitor.' Mr Silly walked in to gasps of amazement from the younger children. He sat on the piano stool, an eight foot vision of green white and gold and in a gruff voice read the story. Then with a cheery wave he waddled out never to be seen again. The children were thrilled! Who could it have been? They knew it could not have been the *real* Mr Silly; he only lived in books. One little girl told her mother she had guessed his identity. "At first I thought it was Mr Collins" (the care-taker) "but his feet were too small. Then I realised. It must have been………the Pope!"

Did the nuns long for love and family life? I cannot say, but I do know that several of them longed for colour. I often needed costumes for my Productions and they were always willing to sew for them. I once choreographed a dance to the words of the Magnificat and wanted the girls to wear black leotards and blue circular skirts. "What shade of blue would you like?" asked Sister Josephine, our Head Teacher. "Oh Josephine!" exclaimed the Mother Superior, "Our Lady blue of course. We'll go to Romford Market on Saturday morning." They duly went to Romford, and bought a bale of 'Our Lady blue' crimplene; enough for a skirt for every girl in the class with some left over for the little Mary in the Infant Nativity Play.

Of course the nuns wore habits, a navy pinafore dress over a blue blouse and a navy veil to the shoulder. It never changed so I was surprised to go to the staff room one day and discover a new nun wearing a brown pinafore dress, a cream blouse, no veil and a tiny suspicion of blusher. She told me she had been to an 'Empowerment' weekend and someone from 'Colour Me Beautiful' had advised the nuns on colour therapy. "I am a 'Warm Autumn'", she informed me. "I should not wear navy blue. It drains me of my natural colour". Gradually other nuns began discreetly to wear different colours and eventually they gave up wearing formal habits, choosing instead to wear a plain wooden cross.

In time a large hall and a modern kitchen were added to the school. Delicious meals were cooked by one of the parishioners, a Spanish lady. A devout Catholic, she always served a fish meal on Fridays. Sometimes it was Fish Pie but this Fish Lasagne is a very good alternative.

Fish Lasagne (for 6 people)

Ingredients

700g (1½lbs) mixed fish such as cod, salmon, smoked haddock
6 sheets lasagne
1 pint white sauce, either home-made or from a packet
50g (1oz) grated cheese (optional)

Method

Cook lasagne in boiling water for ten mins until tender.
Cut the fish into bite size chunks and poach for 5 mins in milk.
Make a white sauce.
Grease an oblong pie dish.
Assemble Lasagne in layers as follows:
- White sauce
- Lasagne
- white sauce
- fish.

Repeat twice more finishing with a layer of white sauce.
Sprinkle with grated cheese and bake for twenty minutes at 180ºC (gas mark 4).

An Awfully Big Adventure

It was summer of 1980. My husband and I and our children aged 11 and 9 had been invited to spend two weeks in Corfu sharing a large tumble-down villa with some London friends and several other families. Instead of flying we had decided to drive down through Europe and catch the ferry from Brindisi. It was going to be 'An Awfully Big Adventure'.

My husband was a seasoned traveller. He had driven over 10, 000 miles on a scooter through Africa, so the thought of about 2,000 through Europe did not daunt him. We planned to visit friends in France, Holland and then Southern Germany, but most of the time en route we would be camping. Therefore, we packed our large frame tent and all our camping equipment in the boot of our old estate car. As poorly paid teachers we had always driven second hand cars, often sold to us by the parents of my husband's pupils. To begin with the children had a lot of extra luggage under their legs. After the first couple of nights camping it proved so complicated repacking everything into the car that the two back seats were laid flat and the children lay on top of the luggage. Poor children; they had a wonderful view of the roof of the car and if they rolled over they could see the scenery out of the rear window.

All went well through France, Holland and Germany. Then, travelling through Austria towards Italy the car developed a tendency to pull slightly to the right. My husband threw the European atlas into my lap, "Find me a route through Italy that doesn't take too many turnings to the left" he commanded. This was a tall order. It meant we could not visit Florence or Rome as they both required left turns off the motorway.

"I long to see Italy!" I cried. "Stop fussing and look out of the window" he replied.

The children were uncomplaining, – both bookworms, they were happily absorbed in their books, quite unaware that the roads to the High Renaissance were flashing by.

We travelled the length of Italy from North to South and eventually reached Brindisi with three days to spare. The camp site was spotlessly clean. It had a swimming pool, a laundry and a very good restaurant.

After three days eating and relaxing around the pool we caught the ferry to Corfu. There was a swimming pool on board the ferry and my daughter thought she would like to go for a swim. As she floated in the salty water she asked me, "Mum, how deep is this pool?" Oh as deep as the sea I joked." She catapulted from the pool like a bat out of hell and was not amused. Our friends, whose holiday villa we were sharing, could not believe we had come all that way in such an old car and added "How do you plan to get home?"

The return journey? That is another story.

Pomodori Ripieni
(Stuffed tomatoes)

Ingredients
4 large tomatoes
Scant 75g (6oz) rice
30g (1½oz) butter
Grated rind of a lemon
30g (1½oz) parmesan cheese, grated
A pinch of nutmeg
Fresh basil leaves finely chopped
Salt and pepper to taste

Method

Heat oven to 180°C, gas mark 4

Cut a lid from each of the tomatoes. Scoop out the pulp, chop and set aside.
Sprinkle salt into empty tomato shells and turn upside down to drain.
Cook rice in boiling salted water until al dente, about 10 minutes.
Drain rice and add butter, lemon rind, Parmesan cheese, seasonings and herbs while the rice is still warm.
Pile into tomato shells.
Put the lids back on and bake for 30 minutes.
Serve warm.

An Awfully Big Adventure

Party Fun

On a recent visit to a well-known cinema complex in Ipswich I spotted a room with the notice 'Fun Room' on the door. A glance inside the finger-smeared glass doors revealed bright carpets covered in popcorn, low plastic tables and chairs and a waste bin overflowing with paper cups and sweet wrappers. I asked what the room was for and was told that it was the children's 'party fun room'. Parents could bring a group of children to the cinema for a birthday treat and hire this room afterwards for a feast of cake and popcorn washed down with cola. Fun indeed!

An article in the Guardian reported that the average party bag taken home from a child's birthday bash costs a stunning £15. While 11million people are surviving on less than £1 a day, this seems obscene. What a strange world we live in. Many parents in the U.K. feel a great deal of pressure to give bigger and better parties for their offspring. How very different from the simple birthday celebrations I enjoyed in my childhood over 50 years ago.

I remember my sixth birthday party in April 1949. Food was still scarce but my grandpa was a master baker and made me a beautiful birthday cake with yellow chicks and my name in icing. I had fourteen friends and cousins to a special birthday tea. There were games in the best sitting room followed by tea and then a photo of us all in the garden. In those days little girls still wore party dresses. Mine was blue velvet passed down from my cousin Elizabeth. I loved it, but would have preferred red velvet. Sadly younger sisters or cousins cannot be choosers!

When my own children, now in their forties, were young I followed the example my mother had set and always had parties in my own home. The format was the same every year. I would make a novelty cake (a train for my son, a Pierrot cake for my daughter) whilst the party food was made by my husband and me working as a team. The Birthday Cake was brought in with the candles alight, the Birthday Boy or Girl blew out the candles and then everyone went back into the sitting room for some calm sitting down games while an adult cut the cake into slices for the children to take home in a paper napkin. This was the origin of the 'party bag' which now costs on average of £15. In time mothers began to add a little token to the piece of cake. It was very small; a tiny present like a hair slide for a girl or a toy soldier for a boy. Like all tiny tokens there was a tendency for this to get out of hand and the party bag escalated to something altogether out of keeping for a children's party.

Our son's friends still talk about their favourite party. It was a 'Tramp's Supper' to celebrate his 13th birthday. Why did it leave such an impression? It can hardly have been the food, which was baked beans and sausages; nor the venue, which was our back garden near the compost heap. No. What they remember with such amusement and affection was the part where Mrs Wheatley dropped all the sausages on the grass and Mr Wheatley shouted at Mrs Wheatley! That was the best fun ever and it certainly didn't cost £15 per child.

These Chocolate Crispies will please the fussiest child and are dead simple to make.

Chocolate Crispies

Ingredients

A large bar of good chocolate
About 110g (4oz) of cornflakes

Method

Melt the chocolate over hot water until runny and smooth.
Cool for 5 mins.
Stir in enough cornflakes to absorb the chocolate.
Put a dessert spoon of mixture into bun cases.
Eat when cold.

Temper in Thailand

It is considered highly improper to show anger publicly in Thailand. This is not a problem for most tourists but my husband and I are known for occasional loud flare-ups. The French find it quite charming. Once, when we were having a particularly explosive row in a side street in Calais a group of men drinking in a nearby bar broke out into a spontaneous round of applause. But you can't do that in Thailand.

We were in one of the many temples in Bangkok. Ted had been filming all morning and he had got some wonderful shots on our new video camera. I always get the camera ready. He hasn't quite got the hang of that yet. Ted does the actual filming.

"There is some excellent footage in here, " he informed me, "but there is a message on the screen that I can't quite read; I do hope that the battery isn't running out."

I charge the batteries. Ted hasn't quite got to grips with that yet, but I was sure it had been fully charged.

"May I have a look through the viewfinder?" I said. "Perhaps I'll be able to read it".
He passed the camera over. I read the message. It said 'No cassette.' He had done two hours filming without a film and it was my fault. I look after that side of things you see.

I wondered how best to tell him. We were in a temple, surrounded by monks. The emerald Buddha was looking down on us. Surely the best thing was honesty. Honesty tempered with a bit of grovelling and a speedy exit. I told him. He went silently white with rage and followed me out of the temple.

"Don't get angry, Ted", I said. "Remember we are in Thailand." "What do you mean don't get angry!, " he replied. "**You** make the mistakes and **I** am supposed to keep my temper. When we get home I am going to learn how to use this camera and I will *never let you touch it again*!"

"Great!" I said. "Is that before or after you have got me to show the film on the television screen?" I always have to look after that side of things you see as Ted hasn't quite got the hang of it yet.

We went back the next day with a cassette in the camera and he filmed it all again. And to show that he had forgiven me for my little lapse Ted treated me to a massage. The temple we had visited, Wat Po, is famous for training people in authentic Thai massage. I don't know whether Ted paid the man to give me a good going over or whether it was delayed guilt, but the next day I was covered in purple bruises. We flew to one of the islands, Koh Samui, where we spent most of the time in bathing costumes, so my bruises were very evident. Lots of people said laughingly, "Has he been beating you?" To which I replied, "Only by proxy".

We had so much delicious food in Thailand that I had difficulty choosing a recipe. I decided against the local breakfast speciality of "Crap [sic] with Sweet Sauce" as I expect you all know how to make crêpes! We had fried plantain from street sellers and on the beach we often ate spring rolls cooked in front of us or sweetcorn baked and served with oil and salt. Our favourite foods were the many different kinds of fish brought up in the catch each morning. On one of the days we went to a Thai cookery course and I learned to make Klouy Buaod Chee (Bananas in Coconut Milk), I hope you enjoy it.

Bananas in Coconut Milk

Ingredients

575ml (1 pint) of coconut milk
275ml (½ pint) water
½ tsp salt
4 chunks ripe banana
110g (4oz) sugar

Method

Combine the coconut milk, water, sugar and salt in a large saucepan.
Bring to the boil.
Add bananas, then reduce heat and simmer uncovered for 5 minutes or until bananas are partially soft.
Cool to room temperature.
Serve bananas in bowls with the sauce.

Temper in Thailand

Good Neighbours

What does it mean to be a good neighbour? We were recently on holiday in Tenerife and met a delightful Norwegian couple, Dag and Astri, who were staying in an apartment near us. We had a lot in common. Dag who had worked for the United Nations, was interested in discussing World Federalism with my husband. We joined them for drinks on a couple of occasions and we also went out for dinner together. Although they liked us as individuals, they had little time for the English.

"Your emissions are polluting our lakes and killing off our trees, " Dag told us, "You English are bad neighbours".

We have had a variety of neighbours over the years. Our first marital home was a tiny terraced house in Teddington with no front garden and a tiny yard at the back. On one side was a strange old widow called Emmie. She had suffered terribly and had been beaten by her husband. It had left her with a great fear of authority and when she had to go to court for non-payment of rent I went with her to hold her hand. When the magistrate entered she turned to me, face close. "Is my breath bad?" she said, rather too loudly. The magistrate treated her with courtesy and kindness. I remember that, when our son was born, she crossed his palm with half a crown- truly the widow's mite.

On the other side, there was a neighbour called Nancy. She was large, menacing and absolute boss in the home. Sometimes she looked after her toddler grand-daughter. "Shuddup! You'd wake bleedin' Jesus Christ you would!" she bellowed, as she soothed her grand-daughter to sleep.

She believed all old wives tales and warned me against putting the baby outside in his pram for a morning nap - very much de rigueur in the sixties. "Ooh, don't put 'im outside. If 'e gets ill in the first six weeks the 'ospital won't take 'im back!"

She also warned me that there was a poisonous plant growing next door to her and she feared the spores might fly over and harm us all. "But Nancy, surely that is rhubarb gone to seed", I said. "No, that's not rhubub. Rhubub crowns; it don't go to seed".

We are all neighbours in today's world. When my husband travelled around the world on a scooter he was given kindness by strangers whom he never saw again. There was the man in the Persian Desert who removed his gloves and gave them to Ted who had none. He probably saved him from frostbite, but we will never know his name. There was the young bank clerk in the Bank of India who gave Ted the equivalent of £5 from his wallet as Ted's letter of credit had not arrived and he had no other funds. His only proviso was, "Please send it to me when you reach the next bank". It meant Ted could eat and buy petrol.

Now we try to help travellers in a similar position. On several occasions we have invited Dutch students to pitch their tents in our garden when they have been unable to find somewhere suitable to camp. We gave a stranded lorry driver bed and breakfast when his vehicle broke down on our road in a blizzard. We really have tried to reciprocate to strangers, but our village is low on needy foreigners.

The Flannigans might complain about the giant heap of manure, which their neighbours have delivered every few years. It makes a mess and is unsightly and smelly. Two doors away Jane and Mark could complain about the bonfires their neighbour lights.

Who lives between these two uncomplaining couples? Oh dear! We do!

Every Christmas we invite our neighbours in for a Yuletide drink to apologise for all our misdemeanors throughout the year. There is plenty of mulled wine and as well as the usual fare of sausage rolls, mince pies and pigs-in-blankets I usually serve cheese straws made to my friend Diana's recipe. I hope the party will give us leeway to sin for another year.

Cheese Straws

Ingredients

225g (8oz) plain flour
225g (8oz) butter
225g (8oz) strong grated cheese (I use strength 4)
1 egg yolk

Method

Rub butter into flour.
Add grated cheese and salt and pepper to taste.
Bind with an egg yolk, knead lightly and chill dough for an hour.
Roll thinly and cut into straws.
Bake for 10 mins on a greased baking sheet at 190ºC (fan 180ºC), gas mark 6.
Leave to cool, then lift carefully with a palette knife.
These keep well in an airtight container.

The Last Straw!

Visit to Japan

In 1994 my husband was invited to make a Lecture Tour of Japan and I was fortunate in being able to accompany him. He was asked to speak to various Conferences organised by the World Federalist Association of Japan. Ted was Chairman of the British World Federalist Association, a much smaller group than its Japanese counterpart.

Before travelling I borrowed a book from the Library on customs and cultural life in Japan. I learned that it was customary to exchange small gifts and business cards. We took some tea towels depicting scenes from our village and had some business cards printed.

The five star hotel in Tokyo was very grand by our standards. In those days we mostly stayed in B&B's or small, friendly Pensiones. On the huge bed there were two kimonos and a pair of slippers each. A pot of green tea was ready for us. The loo was interesting. It doubled up as a loo and a bidet so that after you had "been", jets of warm water and warm air came shooting up. My French friend later remarked, "Oh! How typical of the Japanese to *completely* misunderstand the function of a bidet".

The next morning we were met by the first of our guides, Koichuro Yamaguchi. He presented Ted with his card and me with a little bell to hang on my handbag. "Now we won't lose you, " he smiled. This summed up the attitude to women in the Japan of the nineties. I was a pretty little appendage who ran along behind, jingling. We visited Nara, Ise, Osaka, Hiroshima and Tokyo with several different guides. Ted gave a lecture in all of these cities. My favourite venue was Ise where we attended the religious conference of the Japanese World Federalists. This was held in a large wooden Shinto temple which was open to the elements. Later, Ted and I went outside the temple and we each planted a tree in the sacred wood. Every twenty years the trees from this wood are cut down and the temple is rebuilt exactly as it was before

When we visited Ise temple, we saw some fascinating temple dancing. The movements were very stylised and quite unlike any form of dancing I had learned in the West. We saw many men and women in national and religious dress at the Ise temple and ate a formal Japanese meal. Food was elegantly served in individual oblong or square shallow, lacquered bowls – rice or fish in one, sweet omelette in another. In front of us were chopsticks and small round pots with soy sauce and a squeeze of wasabi paste.

We went on to visit Osaka University. Before the lecture, we were invited to meet the Chancellor of the University. He had a huge, impressive office with a large, carved desk. "Welcome, Mr Wheatrysan" he said. "Here is my card." Ted bowed and presented his card. He then turned to me and said, "Welcome, Mrs Wheatrysan, " and he gave me his card. Oh dear! I had no more of my cards. They said, 'CAROLE WHEATLEY, *Registered Teacher of the Royal Academy of Dancing.*' Unfortunately, I had run out of those cards the night before. What should I do? There was nothing for it but to present him with my other card, the card which said, 'Carole Wheatley. *Bed and Breakfast in the heart of rural Constable Country.*' I still wonder what he thought.

On our last night Mr Yamaguchi and Mr Kawamura took Ted and me out to a Tempura Bar in Tokyo. As we walked along the wide streets Mr Yamaguchi kept indicating small side roads and saying, "Wheatreysan! Up there are girls!" Then, with a shrug towards me, he would say, "But not for you *this* time." In the Tempura Bar we sat on high stools at the bar and had bibs tied around our necks. We were able to watch the chefs preparing and cooking all the courses. We ate cuttlefish, conger eel, scallop, shitake mushrooms; baby egg-plant; lotus root and asparagus. These were all dipped in tempura batter, deep fried and served with delicious dipping sauces. With the meal we drank the sweet rice wine, Sake. Traditionally, when you drink this wine you raise your glass and say, "Bansai!" This means, "May you live a thousand years!"

We had many delicious foods in Japan but I have chosen to give you Tempura.

Tempura Batter

Ingredients

Either make your own or make up according to instructions on the packet.

Dipping Sauce

25g (1oz) fresh root ginger peeled and grated
4 tbsps sake or dry sherry
3 tbsps soy sauce
A little wasabi mustard

Method

To make the dipping sauce, mix together all of the ingredients, then add ¼ pint hot water.
Chill while preparing other ingredients.
Cut fish, prawns, aubergine and cauliflower florets into bite sized pieces, dip into batter.
Heat oil in a deep fryer or deep frying pan until a small piece of bread floats.
Deep fry the tempura a few at time for five minutes.
Drain on kitchen paper.
Serve the Tempura with the dipping sauce.

A visit to Japan

Just say "NO"

So there we were scooping up our Tzatziki by the side of the hotel pool in the delightful village of Petriti. Not that we were staying at the hotel. Our accommodation was further away and decidedly more downmarket. Taking a holiday in Petriti with our friends, Jane and John, was like plunging your hand into a bran-tub, or your spoon into a trifle. You do not know what you will find there. Jane and John knew all their guests, but the guests did not necessarily know each other and the mix was eclectic; a good preparation for loving your neighbour, whoever she or he should happen to be. Jane had rented out two houses (as she has done for the past twenty years) and invited various friends to sample the Mediterranean in August.

This year the party consisted of Ted and me, Jane and John, four other women of a certain age and their offspring, ten in all, aged 16 to 18. I thought it would be interesting getting to know these young people, but our hours hardly ever coincided. They danced, drank and played cards until the small hours, then got up at around mid-day. Ted and I went to bed at midnight (this was considered stuffily early) and got up at about 8 am to go and buy fresh bread for breakfast. We didn't often do things in a large group, there were too many of us, but on our fourth night Jane suggested a trip *en masse* to the nearest hotel, a short bus ride away. This was a luxurious place with air conditioning, a swimming pool, beautiful grounds and Greek Dancing on Wednesday nights. The Retsina flowed fairly freely and most of the party got a little tipsy. I do not drink so I stayed very sober drinking Lilt, and Sue and I shared a bowl of Tzatziki.

It was fun but rather tame for the young who started to jump in the pool. This was a bit much for some of the German residents who did the German equivalent of 'tut tut'. At about ten o'clock one of our "young", a strikingly handsome seventeen year old called James, came up to me and said, "I am just about to throw you in, do you mind?" I said, "Yes James, I do mind," but I realised that I had no chance of staying dry and I found myself being led to the pool and pushed in fully clothed. Once in I struggled out of my dress and with a great sense of release swam around the pool in my underwear. Some instinct had made me put on my best black bra and pants. It was such fun that I got out and jumped in again a couple of times. This was the first time I had ever paraded in my underwear and I found it oddly releasing. It was a great bonding experience for the women of our party. We had not known each other very well until then and suddenly we were swimming around in our Lovables feeling seventeen again. "Isn't this pretty!" said Jane. "We look just like mermaids!" Other people were thrown in. Two large Greek girls stood fully dressed in the shallow end smiling blissfully. "Is it your first time?" I asked. They smiled and nodded sheepishly. "Me too," I said. "But hey! It's great, isn't it?"

The next morning I woke up and wondered why I felt strangely light-headed. Then I remembered. For years I had been a sober, restrained sort of woman and last night for a few minutes (about four actually) I had joined the gang. I was liberated! I was daring! I was bad! I dressed quickly and went to see if any of the others were around. There was Sue at the breakfast table with Jane and Mo and Anna all looking a bit the worse for wear. "Wasn't it fun last night?" I ventured. "Wasn't what fun, darling?" asked Sue. "You know, doing that thing in the pool," I said rather lamely. "Doing what in the pool?" asked Mo. I didn't dare go on. They had obviously been too drunk to remember what they had done in the pool whereas I had no excuse. I was sober. I remembered my Mother's advice all those years ago. "Just say 'No' and mean it Carole." How I wished I had remembered that advice the night before!

Tzadziki

Ingredients

1 large cucumber peeled and diced
1 large pot of Greek Yoghurt
2 tablespoons of mint, chopped finely
Salt and pepper
A dash of lemon juice
2 cloves of garlic, crushed
1 tablespoon of olive oil
1 tsp white wine vinegar

Method

Combine all the ingredients in a bowl reserving a little of the mint.
Pour into a serving dish and chill for an hour before serving.
Add a sprig of mint for colour and serve with pitta bread.

Just Say "No"!

The Cyprus Experience

When my husband retired from teaching, we were no longer tied to the school holidays and were able to take our holidays "out of season." Our first experience of this was a touring holiday in Spain and the South of France. It was the most depressing holiday of my life because I like to be 'where it's at' and we were decidedly where it was not 'at.' At one of the campsites in Spain we were the only residents on the site. The shop was closed. The pool was unheated. The restaurant was no longer operational. But worse still the lights in the toilet and shower room were on a time switch so that when you had been in for five minutes, you were suddenly plunged into darkness.

After a couple of weeks I begged to go home, thinking that, if this was retirement I thought I would rather be dead. To this Ted said, "Perhaps we had better look into package tours further afield". So he booked us into a 4-star hotel in Cyprus in November. We were assured that there would be plenty of sun at that time of year. And people. There would be plenty of people.

We arrived very late at night and reached our hotel in the small hours of the morning. I was rather slow getting off the coach; this meant that Ted was ahead of me in the queue for checking in and I wouldn't push in, to his intense annoyance. As we got to our room, Ted put the key in the lock but it wouldn't turn. "You try", he said. I tried. He tried again. We were marooned on our hotel landing in the middle of the night. Ted started to use brute force and, at that moment, the door was opened from within by an irate Greek man wearing nothing but a glower. Ted had been trying to enter the wrong room.

On our first evening there was 'Cabaret Night' and Ted said, "Cabaret! There might be some dancers. I think we ought to go, darling." Ted's idea of a really good evening is to watch dancers. When we first met I was at a dancing college in London. I do not think Ted has ever quite forgiven me for turning from a dancer to a woman who reads. Anyway, we rolled up to 'Cabaret Night'. Our only entertainers were Pat and John. No dancers. Nothing young and pretty for Ted to leer at. John and Pat were very good singers. Towards the end of the evening John dressed up as Tom Jones and did a very funny imitation of him. "*It's not unusual to be loved by anyone. Ba-da ba-da ba-da.*" Ted was bewildered by this. "I thought Tom Jones was a character from a book, Carole". Ted is very square. The only pop song he knows is "Moon River" because that was playing the night we fell in love.

Anyway, John sang a Tom Jones song and Pat came around the audience looking for men to go up on the stage and join in with him. Ted was aghast. "Please don't catch her eye! I can't go up there!" But she *did* see Ted and she *did* choose him to go up on the stage along with several other protesting men. She introduced them all by name. One was a foundry worker from Corby called Bill. Then Pat said. "Right lads! Put one 'and in the air and one 'and on yer belly." ('Belly' of course was a euphemism for rude parts but luckily Ted didn't realise that.) " Now lads, I want you to join in when we all sing "Ba-da ba-da ba-da". Ted and the others gamely joined in looking very sheepish and I thought, "Oh poor darling!" But there was nothing I could do to help him. I looked around at the audience. The older women were clearly enjoying this display. I even wondered if any of them would throw their underwear at him, but most of them looked as if they were wearing tight roll-ons which would have made this difficult. Ted's performance earned him some notoriety and everywhere we went older women called out, "Hello Ted! Liked your Tom Jones impression. Ba-da ba-da ba-da." They would laugh lewdly and gyrate their hips. Ted took this quite graciously but flatly refused to go to any other 'Cabaret Nights'.

One of the bars served very good snacks for all its customers. I am giving you their version of Hummus here. Whenever we eat it I think of Ted's Tom Jones impression and smile.

Hummus

Ingredients

1 tin of drained chick peas
2 fat cloves of garlic, crushed
The juice of a lemon
A large glug of good olive oil
1 tablespoon of Tahini (sesame paste)
A dash of cumin

Method

Whizz all the ingredients together until smooth and serve with extra olive oil and warm pitta bread.

Tom Jones Impersonation

Shopping in Prague

When Ted and I had been married 25 years, we celebrated by taking a holiday in Prague which, in 1993, was a comparatively new place to visit as a tourist. We arrived in the middle of the night and took a taxi to our hotel, in the centre of Prague. It didn't look much like a hotel from the outside and our bedroom was a shock, as there were neither running water nor curtains in the room and the only towel provided was a small white huckaback hand towel between us. We found communal shower and lavatory facilities along the corridor and were glad to fall into bed.

We were awoken after about an hour by slamming doors, shrieks of laughter and a few snatches of song. We recognised the sound of course. Part of the reason we had gone away was to escape from that sound. It was the sound of young people having fun. Ted gave a little groan and rolled over. "I'll never get back to sleep," he assured me. But, of course he did. At last the unknown young people fell silent and we drifted off. I was awoken a few hours later by what sounded like a giant train hurtling towards the hotel, there was a smashing of glass and a crashing of doors. As I came fully awake I realised that what I was hearing was demolition work just outside the hotel. Ted and I had a serious discussion. Should we contact our tour operator and ask to be moved to another hotel? We decided that we would stay put because we could be moved somewhere else that would be just as noisy and less convenient for the "sights". We later found that our hotel had previously been an extension of the police station used to interrogate prisoners, almost certainly under torture. A small room in the basement bore the notice, "Vaclav Havel our President was held here". We knew none of this when we booked.

We loved Prague. Charles Bridge was beautiful, bustling with life and there was music everywhere. I particularly remember two women singing a classical duet on the bridge. They were blind and were reading the music in braille. Their fingers flew across the page. While there, Ted gave a talk to a group of students at Charles University and we visited Wenceslas Square. We saw Vaclav Havel's house which is very modest for a Prime Minister's residence, and we also went shopping. Ted had only bought one pair of sandals with him and had planned to buy another pair in Prague. "There will be some wonderful bargains," he assured me. After a few days the sandals, which were nearing the end, broke so he threw them away and we went into a department store to buy some more. They were indeed very cheap, but were they a bargain? Would they last? Ted was sure they would be perfectly adequate and bought a pair. We bought a suitcase too.

Two days later the strap on one of the sandals came unstitched. "We must take them back at once, " I insisted. "We can't take them back!" cried Ted. "This was the Eastern Block; they do not know about market forces." So he fixed the offending strap with sticking plaster.

I insisted we take them back. Ted came with me looking very embarrassed and struggling to wear the offending sandal. When we got to the shoe department, there was a tiny difficulty between the shop assistant and me as we had no common tongue. I have never let a little thing like language get in the way of communication so I mimed what had happened and kept saying, "Kaput!" She indicated that she wanted the receipt, which we had lost. At last she ordered Ted to take his shoes off and ushered me to another part of the store.

Poor Ted felt naked sitting there in his socks, but what could I do? I truly felt that taking those sandals back was my contribution to dragging the Czech Republic into the West and possibly one day into the European Community. It was a mission! The sandals were replaced after a very long and uncomfortable wait for Ted.

Before leaving the store we visited the store's restaurant. Cuisine in Prague was not great at that time but we found that some department stores served very good lunches for travellers on a budget.

We ate warm beetroot for the first time in Prague. I have since been served this in Poland and I believe that the eastern Europeans are more adventurous than we are with this under–rated vegetable.

Incidentally, the sandals broke as soon as we got home. So did the suitcase.

You will find a recipe for Polish Beetroot in 'Pastures New' so I am giving you Beetroot Chutney which is equally delicious.

Beetroot Chutney

Ingredients

450g (1lb) onions, chopped
575ml (1 pint) spiced white vinegar
1,350g (3lbs) cooked beetroot peeled and diced finely
2 teaspoons salt
450g (1lb) cooking apples, peeled, cored and chopped
450g (1lb) white sugar

Method

Cook onions in a little of the vinegar for about 15 minutes.
Add the rest of the ingredients (except the sugar) and just enough vinegar to stop mixture from burning.
Cook gently until soft, stirring from time to time.
Add rest of vinegar and the sugar, stirring thoroughly.
Boil steadily until thick, approx. 20 to 30 mins.
Pour into sterilized jars.
This is best if allowed to mature for at least 6 weeks.

The Kindness of Strangers

I didn't particularly want to go to Fuerteventura. As our plane flew low over the island I noticed that it was really just a bare lump of volcanic rock with very few settlements. I was very glad that I had bought a good book.

"Fuerteventura is known as the windy island, " the Receptionist informed us, "but we don't usually get it as windy as this!" We felt we had probably chosen the wrong destination for our winter break but determined resolutely to make the best of it. I had forgotten to pack the Spanish phrase book, but, as Ted said, you only need phrase books in dire emergencies and we weren't expecting one.

On the fourth day of our visit we took a bus to the north coast of the island. It was hotter there - no wind, and we enjoyed a walk, a sunbathe and a snack at one of the many outdoor restaurants. I had forgotten to take my sun-hat - a mistake, as too much sun on the head doesn't agree with me. That evening, after a particularly rich meal accompanied by the inevitable glass of Sangria I was very sick. I put it down to too much sun and starved for the next twenty-four hours. Unfortunately two days later I felt very ill indeed and became increasingly confused. Ted became a little alarmed and decided to call the doctor. Two doctors came with a very sweet interpreter. I speak no Spanish but at this stage I could barely speak English. The doctor asked me questions like, "What is your name?" "Where are you?" "Have you any children?" To which I could only answer, "I don't know."

I should add here that I am epileptic. I was first diagnosed at the age of fourteen and have been on medication ever since. Apart from the fact that I am unable to drive I have never let the condition spoil my life and have been seizure free for thirty years. I do not remember anything after the doctor's visit but in fact I had two Grand Mal seizures in our apartment and was then taken to the hospital in Puerto del Rosario where I had a further seizure, stopped breathing and had to be resuscitated. Ted told me all this the next day. My first memory was of coming round in a hospital bed. There were needles in my wrist, I was attached to a heart monitor and another device was automatically measuring my blood pressure. There were a doctor and a nurse bending over the bed.

"*What eez your nime?*" asked the doctor, who looked like a learned Pavarotti. "*What eez your nime?*" echoed the nurse.

"I don't know."

"*Where do you leeve?*" (Pavarotti again)

"I don't know, ….but **you** are very handsome"

"*Qué?*"

"I don't know…but **you** (pointing at him) are very handsome."

He looked bewildered and asked the nurse in Spanish what I was saying. She blushed, looked embarrassed and then told him. He gave a derisory snort and left my bedside. I hope that in my non compus mentis state I brought a little happiness to that man. I like to think that he went home and said to his wife. "'*Ey, Maria, you may not fancy me but some weird woman in hospital, who doesn't even know her nime, thinks I am 'andsome!*" Lots of happy laughter and clinking of Sangria glasses.

After three days I was allowed 'home' to my holiday apartment. I was unbelievably weak and could only walk a little way supported by Ted. I met with enormous kindness from the staff at the apartment complex, particularly the manager, who had driven me to the hospital, and the gardener, who had helped to get me into the car. To save Ted cooking, one of the members of staff brought in a large Spanish Omelette for us to eat for supper on my first evening home. Whenever I cook this, I remember the kind people of Fuertaventura.

Spanish Omelette

Ingredients

4 large potatoes, cooked and sliced
4 eggs
2 large Spanish onions thinly sliced
75g (3oz) chopped red peppers from a jar
75g (3oz) grated Cheddar cheese (or similar)
2 teaspoons olive oil
Salt and pepper

Method

Turn on the grill.
Heat the oil in the frying pan and fry the onions until soft.
Remove onions from heat and fry peppers, onions and potatoes.
Whisk the eggs in a bowl.
Wipe out the frying pan with kitchen paper and heat the rest of the oil.
Pour in the omelette with the vegetables and cook gently for about 6 minutes, shaking from time to time to avoid sticking.
Sprinkle the cheese on the top and place under the grill for a few minutes to set.
Turn upside down onto a plate and cut into wedges to serve.
This can be eaten hot or cold.

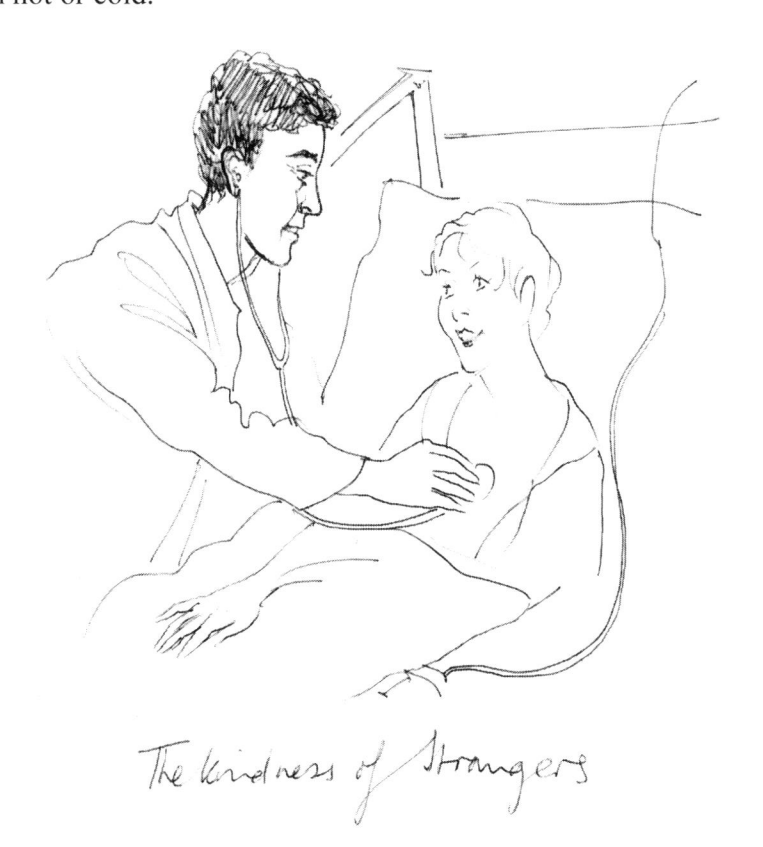

The kindness of Strangers

Pastures New

Shortly after our retirement, my husband and I took part in a Twinning Ceremony between Tendring in Essex and a town in southern Poland called Swidnicka. We don't actually live in Essex; we live in Suffolk. But Swidnicka and Clacton are also twinned with Biberach in Southern Germany, which is where I was born, so we were able to join the coach party from Clacton Sports Centre for the 25 hour journey to, what was for us, 'Pastures New'. We shared our journey with various other people from Clacton and the surrounding villages including a group of line-dancers, who would dance in Swidnicka to give an example of typical English culture.

We stayed with a charming family - mother, father, three lovely boys aged 10, 13 and 16 and a cat called Greg. Pawel, the sixteen-year-old, was our guide as he spoke good English and was very mature for his years. He was very much the man about the house and could turn his hand to most things. On the evening of our arrival I broke the loo which flushed in a peculiar way. I tried to mend it with no success and decided to go and fetch Ted. No need. As I opened the door, there was Pawel. "I hear. No worry. I mend." What else had he heard?

Pawel enjoyed the American cartoon South Park and unfortunately knew all the verses to 'Nanky the Christmas Pooh.' We found the Polish Cuisine a little limited. We love sausage in all its various forms but longed for fresh vegetables, so it was a relief to be offered beetroot. As we boarded the coach to leave, we said to Pawel, "You must come and stay with us in England!" When we got off the coach 25 hours later there was an email waiting for us saying, "I come to you in August, with my cousin Anna, Pawel". We groaned a bit. We hadn't had much to do with 16 year olds for over 12 years, but we got in some South Park videos and planned for their visit.

When they arrived, we hardly recognised Pawel as the talkative boy from Poland. It was his first visit to England and he seemed to be in culture shock. "Young people here have a lot more freedom than in Poland," he commented. He ate everything I cooked and was particularly impressed with my home-made plum jam, so I gave him a jar to take home. The high spot of the holiday for him was not Covent Garden with its colourful street entertainers, nor the state rooms at Buckingham Palace, but visiting Colchester Castle Museum and trying on the chain mail, the slave collar and the toga intended for much younger children. Our museums are apparently much more 'hands on' than the museums in Poland. Pawel's cousin Anna spoke a little more than he did. She had just won a place to an English speaking school and was anxious to practise. She hardly ate anything. She ate toast and fruit for breakfast but refused all food after that, preferring to stay in her room during lunch and supper. She occasionally agreed to gingerly sip a lemon tea at about 9 p.m.

While they were with us, we invited an 'English' Polish family with similar aged young people to supper. I cooked sausage casserole with mashed potatoes and, with a little pressure from Ted, Anna volunteered to make Polish Beetroot. I grew up with a narrow view of beetroot. My mother only ever served it doused in vinegar, which I hated. Ted's mother was a little more daring. She sometimes made a beetroot sandwich with salad cream. I have had Borsch once or twice - but Polish Beetroot is nicer.

The meal was a success and the young all went to the pictures together the next day. We drove Anna and Pawel to Victoria Coach Station and waved them off feeling unsure of how successful the visit had been. Within two days I received an email, "That was the best vacation ever. I really enjoyed the jam. We would like you to come and stay with us soon." Perhaps sometimes our hospitality failures can be more successful than we realise.

Anna's Polish Beetroot

Ingredients

1 large beetroot
2 tbsps sour cream
A little lemon juice
½ tsp salt
½ tsp sugar
A knob of butter

Method

Cook beetroot in its skin for half an hour. Peel and grate into a bowl.
Add all the other ingredients and mix well.
Serve hot.

Pastures New.

Biberach Story

Although I was born in Biberach in Baden-Württemberg I left when I was two and did not return until I was in my mid-thirties. My husband and I together with our children aged 6 and 8 drove through Holland, then to southern Germany, camping on the way.

In Biberach we stayed with Hans Peter and Helga Reiser and Hans Peter's parents. Hans Peter and I were born in the same week, in the same ward of the Kreiskrankenhaus in Biberach in 1943. My mother was a British internee who had been deported from Guernsey in 1942 together with 2, 800 other British born families. Hans Peter's mother and my mother met in hospital and managed to make a connection using French as a common language; Frau Reiser came from Alsace. They had a tall family house in the centre of town with an organ building factory in the grounds. The Reiser family had been building and repairing church organs in the Baroque churches of Baden Württemberg for three generations. We were given a basement flat which included a tiny kitchen and shower room. After a tent this was luxury indeed. In fact the Reisers would never let us cook for ourselves and invited us up for a barbecue most evenings.

In those days very few people in Biberach spoke English. Very few even spoke Hoch Deutsch, preferring to speak Swabish, the local dialect. We communicated through Helga who was only in her twenties and so remembered far more school English than her husband. Since then we have met so many middle aged people who speak very good English that it is easier for us to communicate. I have been learning German for about twenty years but will never be fluent and find the local dialect impossible to understand.

Our first long visit to Biberach was in 2003, when Hans Peter and I celebrated our sixtieth birthdays at the annual Schützenfest in July. This festival lasts for a fortnight with parades through the streets, dancing through the ages, beer tents, children's dancing and a procession called the Jahrgangs Umzug. In this event everyone who was born in Biberach and who is celebrating a 'round year birthday' (30, 40, and upwards) is invited to parade through the streets to cheering crowds. People give you presents and bouquets. Red roses are hung around your neck; gingerbread hearts are proffered. It is very exciting. In the evening you go to an all-night party and finally you are allowed to go to bed.

On New Year's Eve, called Sylvester in Germany, everybody in Biberach stays in and watches 'Dinner for One' on the television. Helga has told me that everyone in southern Germany watches it and my friend Stella, who lives in Holland just over the border from Germany watches it too. It is a ritual that they always observe. It is a two-hander starring two English comedy actors, Freddie Frinton and Mary Warden. Performed in English it takes about twenty minutes and tells rhe story of Miss Sophie, an aristocratic grandee and her faithful retainer, James. It is Miss Sophie's 90th birthday and she is holding a dinner party for her male friends as she does every year. Unfortunately they have all died so James has to serve the imaginary guests and drink their wine so he gets increasingly tipsy. The menu is the same every year beginning with Mulligatawny Soup, "Usual procedure, Miss Sophie?" "Same procedure as every year, James". The final lines are. "I'm tired James. Put me to bed. Usual procedure." To which the rather drunk James replies, "I'll do my best, Miss Sophie".

I think the Germans actually believe that we still eat Mulligatawny Soup, live in grand houses and have retainers called James. But do they think that elderly aristocrats sleep with their servants? Or is it, as I believe, a vast game of sexual role play between a husband and wife? I suggested this to one of my German teachers once and she was shocked.

I have eaten many unusual meals in Biberach; and Helga and I have enjoyed time together in her kitchen. She and Hans Peter visited England for our 40th wedding anniversary and helped prepare the food for a party in the garden. We have swopped many recipes over the years. The dish I am giving is Spätzle. These are egg noodles and they are universally loved in southern Germany. The Reisers eat them on Christmas Day with spicy sausages.

Spätzle

Ingredients

475g (1lb) flour
4 – 5 eggs
1 tsp salt
⅓ – ½ cup water (depending on type of flour)
Melted butter
Hot water

Method

In a large mixing bowl mix flour, eggs and salt.
Add water little by little and keep stirring until smooth.
Beat dough until nothing remains on the spoon when holding it up.
Let it rest for a while then beat again.
Have a pan of simmering water ready on the cooker.
Push spätzle through a dampened potato ricer or a Spätzle board and cutter.
When they rise take the spätzle out with a slotted spoon and toss in hot water to prevent them sticking together.
Serve immediately with fried onions and grated cheese.

Biberach

And the Bride Wore Flip-Flops

It's such a small world these days. Once upon a time a young couple went along to the village church to get married and then off to Brighton or Jersey for a few days honeymoon. Now the world is your oyster - for work, holidays, even weddings.

We once spent two weeks in Sri Lanka. During the first week we toured the 'cultural triangle'. The second week was spent by a beach in the south-west of the country. When we booked ourselves into the Eden Hotel we little realised that it was a wedding holiday hotel.

The Eden Hotel (Adam and Eve, Garden of Eden, geddit?) had a wedding every day that we were there. We became friendly with one bride, Sarah, whose parents and close friends had come to Sri Lanka for the wedding.

"You can bring your wedding dress with you as hand luggage," Sarah told me. Apparently, as long as it isn't too voluminous, you can zip your wedding dress into a polythene bag and an air hostess will hang it up at the back of the aeroplane, just around the corner from the toilets. Most brides find white satin shoes a bit heavy to pack, so they usually plump for pretty flip flops.

The Sri Lankan official marrying them had a limited command of the English language. Sarah was nearly married to her own father in a worrying case of mixed identity. The absence of a priest was more than compensated for by the presence of an elephant. He stood discreetly in the background while the vows were being exchanged. He was even dressed in a maroon velvet cape edged in gold, which bore a marked resemblance to the vestments worn by our rector during Advent.

After the wedding the bride and groom, followed by the wedding party, usually proceed through the swimming pool area to where the elephant is awaiting them. It is difficult to "proceed" with any semblance of dignity when you are being gawped at by ageing tourists on Saga holidays. When the wedding party reaches the elephant he kneels, and the bride is helped onto his back by the elephant's owner. The groom has to manage as best he can and the memory of Sarah's new husband dressed in a white suit, vainly trying to mount the elephant will be with me for a very long time. The elephant is then led on to the beach where he makes a little sortie into the sea. At this stage an ill-assorted crowd usually gathers. With us there were a couple of mystified beach sellers, a badly sunburned German with a digital camera, and a well-spoken couple on a Kuoni holiday who spontaneously clapped and cried "Bravo!" Then it was back to the hotel and everything was over.

That evening newlyweds usually eat their wedding breakfast upstairs in the à la carte restaurant away from the hoi polloi in the downstairs "all-inclusive" dining room. There they pay an outrageous price for a magnum of Champagne. At the Eden hotel all newly-weds are automatically upgraded to the Bridal Suite for one night only. At risk of sounding cynical I do wonder how important the wedding night is to couples who have usually been living together for some time and often have a child to prove it.

Weddings were so different forty years ago. For some of us it was the first time we ever rode in a really grand car. The wedding dress, the visit to the hairdresser and all that went with it were the high spot of our lives. When we walked out of church all our family and friends were there dressed in their best and wishing us luck. I am sure the young people today with their strange weddings have just as many hopes and dreams as we had. Best wishes Sarah, and Nick! May the elephant bring you luck!

Sri Lankan Lime and Coconut Dhal

Ingredients

2 teaspoons of mild curry paste
1 tin of red lentils, drained
1 tin of coconut milk
The zest of a lime plus a little of its juice
Salt and black pepper
A handful of chopped coriander

Method

Gently heat the curry paste in a saucepan and then add other ingredients.
Serve hot with warm pitta bread and a little more coriander for colour.

Canada

In the late nineties Ted and I planned a holiday to Canada, to visit his relations and celebrate our 30th wedding anniversary. We planned to stay with his sister-in-law in Niagara, visit the Stratford Festival, stay in Guelph with a niece and then drive in a hired car up the Bruce Peninsula to Tobermory.

The journey started badly. Half way to the airport, when we had travelled too far to turn back, I suddenly remembered that I had left my make-up bag on the dressing table. "Never mind," said Ted. "You don't need make-up, you look fine to me!" "Well I may look fine to you Ted," I replied, "but it's the others I'm concerned about, I will have to buy myself some make-up at the airport". Ted hates waste. He is careful, almost to the point of meanness, so this started a little row. Despite Ted's protests, when we reached the airport I went to Boots the chemist and bought a basic set of make-up, some cleanser and a newspaper for Ted to read on the journey. "Just time for you to go to the loo before we board," said Ted.

Whilst in the loo I heard our flight being called. In my rush to re-join Ted I forgot that the Boots bag with the make-up and newspaper, was hanging on the loo door. I broke the news very gently to Ted who was furious. "How could you be so irresponsible twice?" he asked.

We were sitting in a block of seats in the middle of the 'plane. There was a little girl of about two sitting in our row, so Ted allowed me to sit next to her, for 6 hours. Her parents had bought her a fluffy toy on the airport but had provided her with neither books nor toys to amuse her on the journey. Hopeless! For the first two hours Ted did not speak to me. He was in an amazing huff! I decided to be charming and gracious to the little girl and amused her with stories and rhymes. I taught her colours from the safety leaflet, you know the sort of thing, "Your oxygen mask will be YELLOW; your lifejacket will be RED."

At 11 o'clock we were served with refreshments. Oh no! I thought. This child is bound to spill her orange juice on me. But she didn't. No! It was Ted who accidentally threw black coffee all over my new cream trousers. Now Freud said there was no such thing as an accident. That may be true; if so I think Ted was psychologically punishing me for forgetting the make-up, twice, and the newspaper. After that he was so sorry that he forgave me and chatted to me all the way to Canada. I was very magnanimous and assured him that the stain would probably come out (it didn't), but with our row behind us, we enjoyed a lovely holiday.

After we had been to Tobermory, we caught a ferry to Manitoulin Island and then drove to Georgian Bay. On the way I saw a beautiful white wolf loping into the woods beside us. I shall never forget that magical sight. We spent Thanksgiving on a small Island on Georgian Bay with the family. Whilst there we were instructed by Ted's sister-in-law to, "Go to the harbour where boats leave for Robinson Island and I will meet you there." Unfortunately, there were 6 different harbours to choose from, but despite the confusion we all met up in the end. We ate turkey with dressing, and a delicious French Canadian meat pie called 'Tourtière'. It has become a favourite part of our Christmas feast. I am giving you Diane's family recipe.

Tourtière

Ingredients
450g (1lb) minced pork
2 cloves of garlic, crushed
1 small onion, finely chopped
Salt and pepper
½ teaspoon savory or thyme
¼ teaspoon ground cloves
½ teaspoon cinnamon
2 cups of water
Dry breadcrumbs (about a teacup)
225g (8oz) shortcrust pastry

Method

Place meat, onions, garlic and seasonings in a large pan and cook, uncovered, for 20 minutes at medium heat.
Cover and allow to rest for 35 minutes.
Add dry breadcrumbs to thicken the mixture.
Correct the seasoning.
Place cooled mixture in a lined pie dish and cover with pastry.
Both pastry and filling must be very cold before the Tourtière is assembled.
Bake at 220ºC, gas mark 7 for 25 minutes.

Canada – White wolf

Lake Garda

For many years I had longed to go on a Great Rail Journey. At last my wish was granted and we planned an organised trip to Lake Garda, with some optional excursions to Verona, Venice and Milan. We were going in June when we could expect sunny weather, but it would not be too hot for my fair skinned husband and as our hotel was beside the Lake, there would be a cooling breeze.

Our first leg of the journey took us from London to Paris, where we stayed overnight in Hotel Mercure. As we had to be at La Gare du Nord Station by 7.00am we had a very early breakfast before meeting our guide at the station. We travelled by TGV through beautiful countryside, passing the Alps then crossing the Italian border through Turin, and on to Milan. From Milan we travelled by coach until we reached our destination in Sirmione, on the southern shore of Lake Garda. Sirmione is an ancient walled town with a little moated castle, the archaeological remains of a Grotto, an interesting museum and, of course, many trattoria and shops in the cobbled streets of the town.

We stayed at a beautiful 4-star hotel with a swimming pool and a ladder into the lake for those who preferred to swim in its sparkling water. Every morning we took breakfast overlooking the lake. A ferry boat operated on the lake and proved a convenient way to visit other towns and villages. One of these was Malcesine, an elegant town with charming cobbled streets. From there we took a cable car to the summit of Mount Baldo and enjoyed spectacular views over Lake Garda.

The tour company arranged excursions to Venice, Milan and Verona. It goes without saying that Venice is very beautiful. Unfortunately, on the day that we were there, three large cruise ships were moored just outside the lagoon. Consequently, the town became so crowded that we were unable to enjoy our guided tour. We decided to escape the busy streets by sharing a water taxi with two other guests from our party. This enabled us to see many of the famous buildings and churches in comfort.

Verona is the setting of several of Shakespeare's plays and one of the highlights of the guided tour was a visit to 'Juliet's House'. This proved to be full of giggling teenagers pretending to snog for photo opportunities. We also visited a Roman amphitheatre where operas and plays are still performed. After some free time to wander at will we were rounded up and boarded the bus for a visit to a local wine cellar. The wines of Valpolicella near Verona are reputed to be some of the best in the region and, after tasting a wide variety, we were in no mood to disagree.

From the wine cellar, we then went into a roomy farmhouse and climbed wooden stairs to the dining room. Jim, one of our group, began to get anxious. "I only eat burgers and sausages," he confided. "This is a real ordeal for me." He had accompanied his friend Paul on this holiday and was only here for the architecture and the art. We were given an assortment of handmade breads and olives to whet our appetites and then ate various vegetable and meat dishes from the area. Even picky eaters could find something they liked and we were served local cheeses and figs afterwards. Each course came with wine and we had a special dessert wine to finish.

I do not remember the names of all the dishes we ate but one of the dishes may well have been Umido alle Cinque Verdure or Meat with Five Vegetables. It is very easy and takes minutes to prepare but it does need quite a long time to cook. It is typical Italian farmhouse cookery.

Umido alla Cinque Verdure

Ingredients

3 tablespoons of <u>olive</u> oil
450g (1lb) of stewing steak or pie veal
1 large tin of chopped tomatoes
325g (12oz) onions, sliced into rings
1 red pepper, sliced
3 or 4 courgettes, sliced
450g (1lb) carrots, sliced

Method

Put the oil in a saucepan; add the diced meat and all the ingredients except the courgettes.
Add salt to taste and simmer in a closed pan for 1½ hours.
Add the courgettes and simmer for a further half hour or until courgettes are cooked.
Serve with rice or baked potatoes and a glass of Valpolicella wine.

Every night in our hotel I drank this delicious cocktail. It was called "Spritz".

Spritz

Mix together ⅓rd Perol or Campari; ⅓rd Prosecco; ⅓rd Soda or Tonic Water.

Lake Garda

The Last Lap

Some of these stories were originally published in a magazine, 'One World,' edited by my husband. Many of them were written much later when I decided I would like to collect them into a Memoir. All the stories are true. We visited all of these places, but of course we also had many other holidays and family experiences. Our honeymoon was spent in Guernsey (where else?) It could have been ruined as our chief bridesmaid arranged for a friend to visit our hotel before we arrived and put sugar in the bed. It did not come out when we shook the sheets and we were too embarrassed to ask for them to be changed.

We have also had two walking holidays which I enjoyed very much. On the first, my husband and I spent two days walking on The Pedder Way in Suffolk and Norfolk. We had hot sunny weather and met only one other person (on horseback) as we trudged this ancient path. It was as if we had stepped back in time. We slept in Bed and Breakfast accommodation each night. Another time we walked The Ridgeway with four friends. It took eight days. We walked ten to fifteen miles a day and it was rewarding but exhausting. Each night we stayed at pre-booked accommodation, eating in local pubs. Our lunches were brought to us each day by our friend Glenda, who was our back up driver.

All these things happened when we were young and middle-aged. In those days we used to sneer at people who took SAGA holidays. How we laughed! Ha ha! "Sexual Advances Gratefully Accepted" we would titter. Now we are very grateful for chauffeur service, porterage, afternoon tea and free alcohol. In fact the leitmotiv at our first SAGA holiday seemed to be, "Mine is a gin and tonic. Make it a double!" On that trip, a second visit to Thailand, we met a rather disagreeable group of people. They were more interested in under-cutting the beach sellers, moaning about the temperature of the food and cheating in the weekly quiz than exploring the cultural sites. On our next SAGA holiday we went on an organised coach tour of Murcia in Spain. That was more enjoyable and we saw some beautiful works of art. The trouble with a group of elderly travellers is that nearly everybody lost something or left something in a hotel safe. Alan dropped his camera in the swimming pool; I lost my moonstone ring; Eileen left her handbag behind at one of the restaurants; somebody else 'came over funny', and mislaid her insurance documentation.

Inevitably, we were eventually drawn to try a sea cruise on a large Fred Olsen ship. We cruised to Norway to see Fjords and Glaciers. We were in an outside cabin with a large window. Sadly funds did not run to a cabin with a balcony. The ship had many dining rooms serving excellent food; there was high class nightly cabaret entertainment plus two dance hosts and a hostess who partnered any solo travellers. The ship boasted two swimming pools with heated sea water. Bliss! On the ninth deck there was a gym with a Jacuzzi. Unfortunately, the dreaded spectre of norovirus hung over the ship. On the cruise before ours sixty people had been taken ill and confined to their cabins. On our cruise we all had to sign a statement saying we had not been ill in the last two days. Every day at noon our captain, whose name was 'Bent', came over the loudspeaker and urged us to wash our hands for at least 20 seconds after every 'visit'. Whenever we entered a restaurant or entertainment area members of the crew would sanitize our hands.

On our first night on the ship the sea became a little rough and I felt sea-sick. I went to the Reception Desk to ask for a sick bag. The receptionist blanched with horror until I assured her I had not yet got my sea-legs and often felt queasy on the high seas. But the rumour was out! Someone on deck six was feeling poorly. Quick! Start a Panic!

This recipe has nothing to do with SAGA holidays or cruises. It is just my favourite recipe. I hope you love it too. Scale it up or down depending on the number of people to be served. Substitute tomato for apple for a different taste.

Sausage Meat Plait

Ingredients

175g (6oz) puff or flaky pastry
175g (6oz) good sausage meat
1 onion, finely chopped
50g (2oz) mushrooms, finely sliced
1 tomato, finely chopped
Salt and pepper

Method

Roll pastry into a wide rectangle.
Mix sausage meat, onions, mushrooms, tomato, herbs and seasoning together in a bowl.
Form into a long sausage shape and lay in the centre of pastry.
Make about 10 sharp incisions in the pastry on either side of sausage.
Beat the egg and paint it on incisions.
'Plait' the incisions over the sausage meat and seal both ends by pinching pastry together.
 Glaze the whole with beaten egg.
Bake for 10 mins at 220ºC (gas mark 7), then reduce to 200ºC (gas mark 6) for about 20 mins.

Last Lap

Profiles

Carole Wheatley

Carole's parents were living in Guernsey when the war broke out. The German army invaded and eventually her parents were taken away to an internment camp at Biberach an der Riss in southern Germany. Carole was born there and spent the first two years of her life behind barbed wire.

After the war the family moved to London where Carole was brought up. She loved dancing and in time went to the London College of Dance and Drama where, in addition to dancing qualifications, she was awarded the L.A.M.D.A Gold medals for verse speaking and acting. She married Ted and had two children in between running a ballet school and teaching drama.

Carole's acting talent was realised when she and Ted wrote and acted in a series of satirical revues that were first presented locally but then moved to the Studio theatre of the Mercury Theatre, Colchester and the Cockpit Theatre in London. They had 5 % of the profits in Beryl Reid's last revue, 'A Little Bit on the Side'.

Holidays have always been important to her and episodes from holidays come out in this book. She loves cooking, using the many herbs, fruit and vegetables grown in their large garden, and has brought back recipes from many of the countries they have visited.

Ted and Carole still live in the East Bergholt home where they brought up their children. She now has many friends in Biberach and gives talks about her early life which strengthens Anglo-German relations.

Sue Bailey

Sue studied life drawing at St Martin's School of Art. She was a master of fashion illustration at Helen Jardine Artists and has been a painter and freelance illustrator for many years. Exhibitions include the Anna Mai Chadwick Gallery, the Langton Street Gallery and the Topsi gallery in New York City.

Carole and Sue go back thirty years. In this book Sue has captured the essence of Carole at so many different ages. Her drawings offer a glimpse of the different episodes in the life that are described in the book.

You can find out more about Sue and her work by visiting her website at http://artbysuebailey.co.uk.